The Ultimate Time Management Toolkit

by the same author

The Ultimate Anxiety Toolkit
25 Tools to Worry Less, Relax More, and Boost Your Self-Esteem
Risa Williams
Illustrated by Jennifer Whitney and Amanda Way
ISBN 978 1 78775 770 7
eISBN 978 1 78775 771 4

The Ultimate Self-Esteem Toolkit
25 Tools to Boost Confidence, Achieve Goals, and Find Happiness
Risa Williams
Illustrated by Jennifer Whitney
ISBN 978 1 83997 474 8
eISBN 978 1 83997 475 5

The Ultimate Time Management Toolkit

25 Productivity Tools for Adults with ADHD and Chronically Busy People

Risa Williams

Illustrated by
Jennifer Whitney

Jessica Kingsley Publishers
London and Philadelphia

First published in Great Britain in 2022 by Jessica Kingsley Publishers
An imprint of Hodder & Stoughton Ltd
An Hachette Company

1

A CIP catalogue record for this title is available from the British Library and the Library of Congress

ISBN 978 1 83997 178 5
eISBN 978 1 83997 179 2

Printed and bound in Great Britain by CPI Group UK

Jessica Kingsley Publishers' policy is to use papers that are natural, renewable, and recyclable
products and made from wood grown in sustainable forests. The logging and manufacturing
processes are expected to conform to the environmental regulations of the country of origin.

Jessica Kingsley Publishers
Carmelite House
50 Victoria Embankment
London EC4Y 0DZ

www.jkp.com

For my goal sponsors:
Zach, Jennifer,
Ezra, and Eden.
Thank you so much!

Contents

Acknowledgments

I really enjoyed the time I spent writing this book and that's because of all the wonderful people who helped with the process: Sean Townsend (editor), Hannah Snetsinger, and the talented team at Jessica Kingsley Publishers, Jane Evans, who edited my last book, *The Ultimate Anxiety Toolkit*, and my incredible book illustrator and friend, Jennifer Whitney. Thank you to my amazing husband, Zach, and my amazing kids, Leo and Max, who inspire me every day. Many thanks for the positivity boosts from Ezra Werb, Eden Byrne, Mike Sonksen, Romy, Anton and Veronica Yanagisawa, Maggie Lynch, Erica Curtis, Miguel Chavez, Camille Brown, Stevon Lewis, Irene Ashu, Dr. Michael Feldmeier, Dr. Scott Waltman, Andrew Ralles, Cynthia Siadat, Andrew Lawston, Michael Ian Scott, Joel Levin, Dulcie Yamanaka, Solomon Carreiro, and Amanda Way, and to editors Chiwan Choi and Catherine Kielthy, who published my wellness articles in *Cultural Daily* and *Breathe* magazine. Thanks to all the wonderful clients and students I've interacted with over the years who tried out and used the tools in this book. Thanks to all of the readers of my self-care posts on Instagram (@risawilliamstherapy) and thanks to Yeukai Kajidori, Trevor Stockwell, Dr. Tarryn MacCarthy, and Dr. Tamara Soles for interviewing me on their podcasts. Thanks to Publicat and Alpina Publishers for translating *The Ultimate Anxiety Toolkit* into other languages.

   And a big thank you to all of readers of *The Ultimate Anxiety Toolkit* for reaching out to me and telling me about your experiences reading the book and using the tools! Feel free to contact me through my website, www.risawilliams.com, and tell me what tools and techniques worked best for you.

Thanks to the empowering influences of authors Martin Seligman, Edward Hallowell, Judith S. Beck, Aaron Beck, Albert Ellis, Thich Nhat Hanh, David D. Burns, Esther Hicks, Brené Brown, Joseph Campbell, Jen Sincero, Marie Kondo, Victor Frankl, and Wayne Dwyer. I am so grateful to have all these positive influences in my life, and I really hope this book gives back a little positivity, too.

Please visit www.timemanagementtoolkit.com for more tools, tips, and exercises.

Visit www.risawilliams.com to read more writing by Risa Williams.

Time to Talk About Time

Do you have a complicated relationship with time? Do you often feel frustrated with time because you "never seem to have enough of it"? Do you feel like time is "slipping away" and that you never complete your to-do list as a result?

The Ultimate Time Management Toolkit provides practical techniques to help you organize your time, find your motivation, achieve your goals, and feel more emotionally connected to your successes. The tools in this book are designed to help you see time as something you can "stretch" by finding the "fun" in the things you have to do, rather than seeing time as something that's "shrinking" because of the stress you're experiencing.

In my last book, *The Ultimate Anxiety Toolkit*, I wrote a little about my own experiences with anxiety over the years, and how this led me to want to create simple anxiety reduction tools to help others who were experiencing the same types of things. Similarly, I hope these time management techniques will feel relatable and easy to use in your everyday life.

My personal relationship with time didn't always go so smoothly. When I was younger, I often felt like I was always running out of time, and to compensate, I constantly raced around from one thing to the next. But no matter how fast I went, I still felt like there was never *enough* time.

By the time I was in my 30s, I was experiencing a high level of burnout. Although I had never been diagnosed with ADHD (attention deficit hyperactivity disorder), I started to realize that I might have a few **attention deficit traits**, a term coined by psychiatrist Edward Hallowell (2005).

For people who have an ADHD diagnosis, or suspect they might have ADHD (which would include having five or more ADHD symptoms for longer than six months and can be assessed by a doctor or a psychiatrist), some common **executive functioning** issues can include trouble controlling impulses or emotions, problems with organizing and planning, trouble focusing on tasks and sustaining attention, losing objects and forgetting things, and trouble prioritizing tasks (see: **Mental Health Resources, ADHD Self-Test**). However, sometimes people who don't have an ADHD diagnosis may experience some attention deficit traits when they are also feeling high levels of stress.

In my case, one attention deficit trait that I often experienced was going into **hyperfocus** for hours at a time, only to crash afterward and feel very anxious as a result. Although I often found myself slipping into this intense state, what I wanted to know was, how could I smoothly get out of hyperfocus when I needed to without all the anxiety and stress? I knew I needed to find some tools to help me do just this!

Around this time, I became a mom, and I was also juggling multiple careers: working as a clinical psychotherapist, running my own practice, writing, and teaching at different universities. I began studying books on productivity and time management as a way to manage my complicated schedule, and as a result, I started to develop tools to stay more organized and focused.

Using productivity tools such as bullet journaling and time blocking, I started to also incorporate strategies from **cognitive behavioral therapy** (which explores how thoughts affect emotions), from **mindfulness** (which emphasizes connecting with the present moment), and from **positive psychology** (which encourages cultivating happiness), along with **stress-reduction** techniques which focus on balancing the mind and body.

In my therapy practice, many of the clients I was seeing for anxiety also wanted help managing their schedules, finding their focus, and accomplishing their goals. I was also seeing many adult clients with ADHD, who were specifically asking for executive functioning tools. My other clients who *didn't* have ADHD or anxiety disorders, who also wanted time management tools, tended to fall under a category I call **Chronically Busy People**.

Chronically Busy People can be parents, entrepreneurs, CEOs, students, people pursuing multiple careers, athletes, artists, performers, professionals—you name it! They come in many different forms, but they have one thing in common: They're always busy. And because of this, they also needed help managing their time as well.

For all of these people with busy ADHD brains or chronically busy lives, they also had many amazing strengths, too. They would often bravely take on challenging tasks, they would often see things from creative and original perspectives, they would often accomplish *a whole lot* of things (despite sometimes telling you otherwise), and they would often courageously step outside of their comfort zones to bring about positive change.

Sometimes, they just needed to realize that these qualities were actually super-powers that they could learn to use more deliberately in everyday life.

When I needed help with time management, I wanted a book that would not only help me improve my productivity, but also provide simple ways to feel less stressed out about the tasks I had to complete. Mostly, I wanted ways to feel better about time so I could spend more of it doing the things I really wanted to do.

It is my hope that the tools in this book will help you start to shift your feelings about time to more positive ones, so that you can create more of it for yourself to enjoy.

You can change your relationship with time by changing your thoughts. And you can change your thoughts...by taking things one small step at a time.

Tips for Using the Toolkit

- These tools are meant to be supplemental and not as a replacement to medical care or psychotherapy. In fact, practicing these tools in addition to other self-care practices can often turbo-boost their effects!

- Take it one tool at a time and go at your own pace. Give yourself a few days to think about each technique and to play around with the idea for a while after you read each chapter.

- The worksheets can help you apply the information in a custom-tailored way to your own life. Writing stuff down on paper generally helps our brains retain the information more, which can really help the new habit stick. It can also be helpful to keep a list of the specific tools in this book that work well for your own unique brain, so that you can revisit them more regularly.

- It's all about percentages. If you only use a new tool a little bit at first, that's great. Tip the balance toward positive patterns one little percentage at a time. Play around with new ideas in small, consistent ways that feel manageable to you. If you're changing things in tiny percentages each week, it can have a big positive impact on your life overall.

It's helpful to remember:

Every small step you take in a positive direction leads you to a different outcome.

CHAPTER 1

When You Want to Manage Your Time…

* The Task Intensity Meter
* The Time Buffer
* The Task Dessert
* The Brain Warm-Up
* The Gear Shifter

THE TASK INTENSITY METER

As we go throughout our day, our stress levels may be rising without us even realizing it…until we're already in a terrible mood! For this reason, it's important to learn what stress feels like as it's rising and what's actually triggering your stress, so that you can take steps to bring it down before it gets too high.

Neuroscience nugget: In a laboratory study done at Georg-August University of Göttingen in Germany, researchers gave two participant groups (ADHD and non-ADHD) a stress test and discovered that, "Consistent with our assumptions in regard to the psychological stress response, the ADHD group experienced significantly greater subjective stress" (Lackschewitz, Hüther, and Kröner-Herwig, 2008).

In other words, if you have ADHD, you just might be *very* sensitive to stress.

Stressors are things that happen to us during the day that trigger our stress. Think of stressors as negative feeling amplifiers, and they can really crank those feelings right up to a 10 (or even an 11)!

While it's easy to identify some stressors—like getting into an argument or running late to an appointment—other times, we might not have noticed what stressors have triggered us. At the end of a long day, we might wonder: "Why am I feeling so stressed out right now? What even caused this?" And there might be a simple answer to this question.

Sometimes, what caused your stress were the tasks you had to do that day and the order you did them in. An easy way to remember this is:

Intense tasks = Intense moods experienced

The Intensity of Tasks

Imagine each task you have to do is a block that's size correlates to how stressful it is for you to complete. When you pile too many big blocks on top of each other without considering how you're stacking them, the task tower is probably going to topple you over, emotionally.

Too many tasks stacked haphazardly = Stress

The Task Intensity Meter is a tool you can use to reduce scheduling stress. With just a little bit of pre-planning, you can keep yourself from emotionally tipping over by stacking your daily task blocks in a much easier way.

Learning how much energy tasks require of you

can improve your emotional experience of time.

Different Intensity Levels

To begin using this tool, imagine a **Task Intensity Meter** with **low, mid** and **high** written on it. **Intensity,** for this purpose, is the amount of **mental energy** required to complete a particular task. To start using this tool, ask yourself: "What types of tasks feel low/mid/high intensity to me?" Or, in other words, "How stressful does this task feel to me to complete?"

Let's take a few typical household tasks as examples and rate them using our **Task Intensity Meter.**

Task example: Taking out the trash

Intensity rating: Low

For most people, this would be considered a **low-intensity task.** Although taking out the trash doesn't feel fun, it also doesn't usually take that long to do, nor does it require much thinking or physical energy most of the time. Most would rate it "low" on the scale. However, if you've waited weeks to take out the trash, this would now raise it from "low" to "high" on **The Task Intensity Meter.** How long you wait to do something changes the intensity of the task.

Now, what might feel more like a **mid-level** task?

Task example: Cleaning out desk drawers

Intensity rating: Mid-level

Cleaning out your desk drawers? Maybe this is more of a **mid-level intensity** task, depending on how jam-packed your desk drawers are and how long it's been since you last cleaned them out. If there are random crumpled papers wedged in there that require extra attention for you to sort, this makes it take a little more time and energy than a **low-level** task. If you discover there's only a few pens rolling around in there and nothing else, you might downgrade this to **low intensity** instead. So, what would a **high-intensity task** possibly look like?

Task example: Cleaning out the garage

Intensity rating: High

For many people, cleaning out the garage might make the meter's needle jump all the way to "high." It might involve a lot of sorting, organizing, and physical maneuvering that might make a person feel stressed to even think about. Maybe you have to lug heavy boxes of stuff out to the curb; maybe you have to battle some spiders. Maybe it's a large task that needs to be broken down into many days of boxes and bug battles. Since the whole thing might take a lot of mental and physical energy to complete, it would probably earn a **high-intensity** rating from most people.

All of these **task intensity** ratings will change depending on whom you're talking to, their current stress level, how much energy they have, and how they relate emotionally to the task ahead of them (not to mention how many spiders they have in their garage).

In other words, it's different for everyone. You have to feel it out for yourself depending on each task that's in front of you each day. After some practice, you'll learn how to rate tasks in front of you more automatically, and how to arrange them in a way that best suits your mental and physical energy.

How Many Tasks Can I Do in One Day?

You might think something like, "I can easily accomplish at least 20 tasks a day!" and perhaps this might be true if all the tasks were **low-intensity**. However, accomplishing 20 **high-intensity tasks** is another story altogether. It's not to say you couldn't do it, but how are you going to feel *emotionally* as a result? Probably not that great!

Tasks cost us different amounts of mental and physical energy depending on how intense they feel for us to complete. In this way, a few tiny **low-intensity tasks** might take the same mental energy as doing one challenging **high-intensity task**.

Often, people use the quantity of tasks they accomplish each day as a way to evaluate their daily performance, and this can trigger a lot of negative self-talk as a result. You might get to the end of the day and beat yourself up because there are still many things left on your to-do list, but this doesn't take into consideration how difficult each of the tasks on your list were for you to experience emotionally.

You can remember it like this:

All tasks are not equal in terms of the mental and physical energy spent.

Instead, try asking yourself: "What's my **daily high-intensity task threshold**?" Observe how tasks affect you emotionally, and collect some data over a few weeks by recording it in a journal. How many **high-intensity tasks** can you do *without* tipping yourself over into a highly stressed-out emotional place? Figure out your **threshold number,** and try to avoid overbooking your schedule by keeping it in mind more often.

Using The Task Intensity Meter

To use **The Task Intensity Meter,** create a task list of upcoming tasks you need to do for the day. Then, rate each task by intensity level: **low, mid, high.**

The way you rate tasks is specific to you and how stressful they typically feel for you to complete. It's different for everyone as everyone feels different levels of intensity depending on what task they need to do, and this can fluctuate daily depending on how much physical energy they have to spend. Here's a sample list from a client who arranged work tasks in a way that felt more "balanced" to her:

Task list	Intensity rating
Answer work emails	Low
Do two pages of work report	Mid
Finish certification course	High
Fill out travel reimbursement	Low
Team meeting	Mid

Here's a sample list from a student who wanted to space out **high-intensity tasks** in order to avoid feeling overwhelmed by the end of the afternoon:

Task list	Intensity rating
Study for philosophy exam	High
Respond to professor's email	Mid
Finish writing art history essay	High
Return books to the library	Low
Go to study group	Low/Mid

One parent client felt "completely crushed" by a packed schedule full of "rushing around to kid stuff" while also trying to maintain "household demands and non-stop errands." The school run was becoming a consistent source of stress to her, so we worked on making sure this wasn't directly followed by yet another **high-intensity task.**

I asked her what felt less intense for her to do after the school run. She decided that going to the grocery store close to her house and doing light cleaning at home felt "a little easier to do." So, we decided to shuffle **high-intensity tasks** with lower ones, and came up with a task order that helped to lower her daily stress:

Task list	Intensity rating
Morning school run for two kids	High
Pick up a few things at grocery store	Low
Laundry or light cleaning at home	Low
Do a few errands after lunch	Mid
Afternoon school run	High
Prepare dinner	Low
Help with homework	Mid
Exercise and stretching (20 minutes)	Low

Get Honest with Yourself About Intensity

During our first discussion of how intense certain daily tasks felt, this client had initially rated the school run as a **low-intensity task,** but after some discussion, she realized that it was stressing her out way more than she thought it was.

"But all I'm doing is driving kids to school," she said, "Other people do it each day and it's easy for them. Why do I feel so tired and drained afterward?"

Maybe it's because you're battling rush hour traffic while trying to deliver your kids to school safely and competing with other parents for the last remaining parking space for miles? Or perhaps it's just that early morning tasks feel harder for you generally? There are dozens of possible reasons why a task like this might feel stressful to a person. It's okay to admit to yourself that you're feeling overwhelmed by a daily task you have to do. Try to avoid comparing your experience to how you think other people are handling the same task.

Considering how we often misread our *own* stress levels, isn't it possible that we might be misreading other people's stress levels, too? Everyone is different, and everyone's energy is drained by different things at different rates, depending on how they are feeling physically each day. The truth is, we really don't know how stressed out other people are by different things.

Focus instead on what you do know: How intense tasks feel for *you* to do. Then, you can find some practical ways to make them feel less stressful to do on a daily basis.

In other words, expecting yourself to have limitless energy and to experience all tasks as **low intensity** ones, is a really unrealistic expectation to have of yourself (or of anyone else).

Give yourself permission to admit that a daily task is feeling stressful for you to complete.

When we give ourselves permission to admit that a certain task feels intense for us to do, it helps us arrange our schedule in a way that helps us, rather than hinders us.

Getting Honest About Hobbies

Getting honest with yourself about **task intensity** can help you schedule your hobbies as well. One client had rated practicing piano as a **low-intensity task,** thinking it would be a relaxing activity to do each day after work. However, after some reflection, he realized that practicing piano really felt more like a **mid-intensity task** for him to do, and that scheduling it after a work day full of **high-intensity tasks** was actually making him feel more stressed, not less.

Instead, he decided to move piano practice to a different time slot, one that wasn't right after a bunch of **high-intensity tasks,** and found that it was much easier to enjoy practicing again. Then, he chose other hobbies that felt **lower intensity** to do on work days instead.

By understanding the emotional effects of **task intensity levels,** you can start to feel more empowered to arrange your schedule in a way that feels more balanced to you.

Practice Rating Tasks

Using **The Task Intensity Meter** tool, map out your daily tasks in a way that's unique to your mental energy to improve how you're emotionally experiencing your time.

Worksheet: Write it out!

Write out 3–5 tasks you want to accomplish. In the column next to the task rate how "intense" this task feels to you emotionally (using Low/Mid/High).

Task	Intensity level
1	
2	
3	
4	
5	

Now, taking into consideration task intensity levels, try to arrange your list in a way that feels more balanced to you:

My re-arranged task list

Task	Intensity level
1	
2	
3	
4	
5	

THE TIME BUFFER

When it comes to completing intense tasks, it's very easy for someone with ADHD to go into **hyperfocus** mode. This is where, with laser-like focus, they zoom ahead toward completing a task, often tuning out much (if not all) of what is happening around them. When they're in this mode, it's easy for them to accomplish a very impressive amount in a very short period of time! However, going into hyperfocus mode can drain their physical and mental energy very quickly, often causing them to experience intense emotions afterward as a result.

It's like blasting a spacecraft into hyperspace. You'll get to your destination in a very short amount of time, but it will require extreme focus not to crash into asteroids along the way. Afterward, the spacecraft might be shaky, and ideally, you'll want to pull over to the first available planet to refuel.

When your daily work schedule becomes overbooked, there is a greater danger of switching into hyperfocus mode too frequently. As writer Reed Brice describes first-hand: "Burning the candle at both ends to make ends meet can be downright devastating to our health, and since we're hyperactive and hyperfocused by nature, we're especially vulnerable to its effects.

It can be difficult to recognize fatigue until we're in deep, though, especially when we live with ADHD" (Brice, 2019).

If you know that you tend to go into hyperfocus frequently, it can be helpful to become more aware of what that mode feels like to you in your body and how it affects you.

What are some warning signs your body sends you when you've been stuck in this intense mode of focus for too long a stretch of time? Do you feel eye strain or do you get a headache? Do your shoulders tense up? Do you start to feel more easily frustrated or short tempered?

Practice observing these body signs as they appear throughout the day, and then, when you start to feel them kick in—it's time for a **Time Buffer** break.

Time Buffers are breaks you can take throughout the day where you deliberately allow your body and brain to reset and you intentionally allow your stress level to come down a notch.

Think of a **Time Buffer** as a mental pause button between tasks. Typically, for higher-intensity tasks, you would need a larger mental pause to reset yourself. For lower-intensity tasks, you would need a shorter mental pause to reset your brain.

For example, here is a schedule with buffer breaks in between sets of tasks:

Task	Intensity level
Meeting with supervisor	High
Long buffer break	
Submitting invoices	Low/Mid
Short buffer break	

You could also visualize it like this:

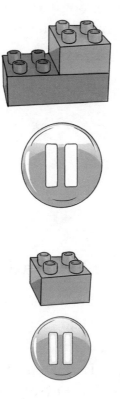

Shorter Time Buffers should ideally be at *least* 20–30 minutes, depending on what tasks you have just completed. **Longer Time Buffers** should be longer than a half hour and take into consideration how much time you will actually need to reset yourself physically, mentally, and emotionally.

Generally, most of us tend to underestimate how long it actually takes for our bodies and brains to relax. It's not uncommon for busy clients to tell me that they only took a few minutes out of the entire day to rest in between racing around. As a result, they often wonder why resting had little to no effect on their mood. This is because it was only for a few brief minutes...out of an entire day. It's quite possible you're going to need a much longer time to really let your stress levels come down a notch, in order to feel better emotionally.

The stress hormones cortisol and adrenaline are released when we have to slog through a mentally exhausting or demanding task. These stress hormones can stay in our bodies for *several hours* after the initial release (Hannibal and Bishop, 2014). So, if you've just completed a difficult **high-intensity task**, it's probably going to take you *at least* an hour or two to fully reset yourself.

Let the Inspiration In

Have you ever been sitting still doing nothing for a few minutes, when suddenly, a new idea just popped into your head? Legendary author Agatha Christie once said she figured out the plots to her books while she was "walking or just washing up" (Thompson, 1966). While doing the dishes, she would let her brain unravel plot twist problems.

Sometimes, our brains need to take a break from the task that's challenging us in order to solve the little mysteries of how to proceed. Answers to problems can form in our brains when we actually relax our minds long enough to receive them.

Neuroscience nugget: Our brains need downtime to process information, store memories, and to generate new ideas. According to Ferris Jabr, author of *Why Your Brain Needs More Downtime*: "Downtime replenishes the brain's stores of attention and motivation, encourages productivity and creativity, and is essential to both achieve our highest levels of performance and simply form stable memories in everyday life" (Jabr, 2013).

So, how can we use our downtime as a way to find more clarity and more focus?

> **Neuroscience nugget:** Meditation has been proven effective to help people lengthen their attention span and sharpen their focus, as Hallie Levine explains, "One landmark UCLA study found that people with ADHD who attended a mindfulness meditation session once a week for 2½ hours, then completed a daily home meditation practice that gradually increased from 5 to 15 minutes over 8 weeks, were better able to stay focused on tasks" (Levine, 2020).

Practicing a short meditation or mindfulness exercise in between tasks can help you gain clarity and find your focus to accomplish what's ahead. There are many ways you can begin to practice meditation on a regular basis. Listening to a short guided meditation for a few minutes can be an easy way to start, and you can find many free guided meditations on YouTube or various mobile apps.

If sitting still for meditations is difficult for you, try doing a walking meditation where you walk around a room (or a yard) slowly in a circle for a few minutes. Practice feeling your feet touch the ground with every step. When your mind wanders, bring your attention back to your feet and how they feel walking on the floor. Find your calm by mentally connecting with each step you take.

Both **meditation** and doing **light exercise** can also be helpful ways to raise your dopamine levels, which can increase your brain's attention and clarity.

> **Neuroscience nugget:** According to psychologist Kelly McGonigal, "When you exercise, you provide a low-dose jolt to the brain's reward centers—the system of the brain that helps you anticipate pleasure, feel motivated, and maintain hope. Over time, regular exercise remodels the reward system, leading to higher circulating levels of dopamine and more available dopamine receptors" (McGonigal, 2020).

Here are some **movement-based Time Buffer** activities that have successfully worked for clients:

* "Going for a short run."
* "Walking my dog."
* "Walking to get lunch instead of driving."
* "Working on the garden in my yard."
* "Dancing in my living room to my favorite song."

Now that you've got some ideas, it's time to write out your task schedule, and plan out a few **Time Buffer breaks** in between tasks in order to de-stress, reset, and let the inspiration in.

Worksheet: Write it out!

Write out 3–5 tasks you want to accomplish. In the column next to the task, rate how intense this task feels for you emotionally (using Low/Mid/High) and arrange them so there aren't too many **high-intensity tasks** stacked up together. In between the tasks, write out: "Break" and write down the **time buffer** that you will do to mentally reset yourself in between tasks. For example:

Sample task list:

Task	Intensity level
Finish work report	High
Break: Do a meditation, go for a short walk	
Answer emails	Low
Break: Sit in the backyard, water plants	
Finish cleaning out cabinets	Mid
Break: Listen to a funny podcast	

☆

Now, try writing out your task schedule and be sure to plan some mentally relaxing breaks for yourself:

My task list:

Task	Intensity level
Break:	
Break:	
Break:	

THE TASK DESSERT

Now that we understand how some tasks feel more intense than others, what's a helpful way to arrange tasks that helps you actually complete them?

In fifth grade, my son had consistently been doing his science and history homework first while saving his math homework for last each day. As he put it, math homework was his "least favorite thing ever" and he didn't enjoy doing it at all, so naturally he wanted to avoid it for as long as possible. The problem was, by the time he had done all his other work, he was already so tired from finishing the other stuff, that math homework was now a super **high-intensity task** to complete, and it was taking him until long after dinner to complete it.

As a result, he started procrastinating about doing his math homework, and the unfinished worksheets were starting to pile up.

You can think of it like this:

Procrastination = Shoots Task Intensity Meter up a notch

If taking out the trash was initially low intensity to you, but you waited two weeks to do it, and now the trashcan was overflowing onto the floor, it's become a **high-intensity task** to complete. Likewise, the math assignments had gone from relatively **low-level** to **high-level intensity** for my son to do.

To a certain extent, we all tend to procrastinate about tasks that don't feel "fun" to us to do, unless we have specifically trained ourselves to do otherwise. For those with ADHD, it can often become a consistent habit to procrastinate and avoid "un-fun" tasks, which then kicks those tasks up to an even **higher-intensity level**.

> **Neuroscience nugget:** In a study done by researchers at Radboud University in the Netherlands, "Individuals with ADHD recalled and executed less of their own real-life intentions. Moreover, there were clear links between everyday prospective memory performance and reported procrastination behavior, and everyday prospective memory performance mediated the link between ADHD symptoms and procrastination behavior" (Altgassen, Scheres, and Edel, 2019, p.59).

You can think of it like this:

$$\text{High-intensity task} + \text{Mental fatigue} = \text{Procrastination}$$

$$\text{Procrastination} = \text{Stress}$$

$$\text{Stress} = \text{Shrinks our perception of time}$$

Now we have taken something "not fun" and made it *even more* "not fun" for ourselves to do in a self-perceived shorter amount of time. It's an anxious loop we've created for ourselves to get stuck in. To get out of this loop, we need to instead find the "fun" again in order for our brains to re-engage.

Save the Fun for Last

Over dinner, I explained to my husband and kids the idea of arranging tasks by **intensity levels** and **mental energy levels** needed to finish tasks.

"What homework feels **low intensity** to you?" I asked my son.

"Pretty much anything other than math," he answered, "Science is okay and I really like history."

"So, maybe you could try to do your math homework first when you have *more* energy to complete it," I suggested. "And save history for last because it's already easier for you to do."

"And then, history homework would be your '**Task Dessert**'!" my husband chimed in, inventing a new catchphrase in our house.

Task Desserts are **low-intensity tasks** that also feel a little fun or a little easier to do.

Task Dessert = The task you save for last
(because it feels easier or more fun to do)

We wrote out a new task list to try:

Task	Intensity level
Math homework	High
Science homework	Mid
History homework	Low – **Task Dessert**

Although my son was really not convinced that *any* of his homework should be called a "dessert," he agreed to test out the new task order. As a result, after only a week, he was consistently completing all of his homework much faster, and was finishing with ample time to spare before dinner.

How might this work for you with your daily tasks? Are there parts of your job each day that feel slightly more fun for you to do than others? How about saving those for last instead of doing them first? Try it out and see how it works for you.

Here are some **Task Desserts** that clients saved for last because they felt more "fun" to do:

* "Worked on a logo design."
* "Browsed new laptops online."
* "Organized desk space and rearranged files."
* "Finished reading an article related to something I'm working on."
* "Learned how to do something new in photo editing software."

Task Desserts look different to everyone, depending on different people's personalities and interests. And even this can change frequently for each person, depending on how much physical and mental energy they have to spend each day. However, generally speaking, saving an easier task for a **Task Dessert** can help us control how stressed out we feel at the end of the day.

Try to end your schedule with a **low-intensity task** each day, and see if this helps your day flow more smoothly into night.

Worksheet: Write it out!

Thinking about your typical day, what are some **low-intensity tasks** that frequently feel more "fun" for you to work on? Write out 1–5 **Task Desserts** you can try to save for last.

Tasks I can save for Task Desserts:

1. . . . .
. . . .

2. . . . .
. . . .

3. . . . .
. . . .

4. . . . .
. . . .

5. . . . .
. . . .

THE BRAIN WARM-UP

Sometimes, when we have trouble engaging our attention on a challenging task in front of us, we might try to force ourselves forward. This doesn't typically work out so well in terms of task completion. Now the task isn't feeling "interesting" any more for our brains to finish, and as a result, our brains want to avoid doing it altogether. For those with ADHD, this is even more of an intense feeling, as they tend to have an **"interest-based nervous system"** that is wired to fully engage their focus on a task they mentally label as "interesting" at the time (Dodson, 2021).

So, what can we do when our brains completely lose interest in a task we need to finish? You can start by using a tool called: **The Brain Warm-Up**, which can help mentally prepare your brain to engage again.

You can remember the tool like this:

Instead of jumping right into a task you have been avoiding,

try doing a Brain Warm-Up first.

Find Your Focus

Before we pick a **Brain Warm-Up** to try, it's helpful to understand the different types of focus. Let's say you're working on a word search puzzle—this requires more acute attention—your focus is now really limited to just scanning letters to find a particular word in front of you.

Just like a camera lens, your eyes and brain have to really zoom in on what you're looking for.

Try this now. Find the word **"TREE"** below:

$$
\begin{array}{llllllll}
F & O & C & U & S & Z & P & H \\
I & N & I & T & I & A & T & E \\
N & G & R & O & W & P & R & L \\
D & O & E & S & N & K & E & P \\
T & A & S & K & I & D & E & A
\end{array}
$$

For those few seconds, your attention and interest were **fully engaged!**

> **Neuroscience nugget:** Why do puzzles and word searches work so well to stimulate our brain's interest? According to writer Lisa Milbrand, puzzles can activate a "rush of dopamine in your nucleus accumbens, the area of the brain responsible for rewards and reinforcement." In addition to the dopamine surge that comes with doing the puzzle, you also get another rush of dopamine when you've successfully completed the puzzle, too. All of this can increase our brain's interest level and make us feel more motivated to move forward (Milbrand, 2021).

When you just did that word search, you probably experienced a **fully focused** state of attention.

The Three Settings

Now let's explore what other **types of attention** feel like to experience. Just like a camera lens, you could think of your attention as having these three settings:

Unfocused attention

In this **unfocused** setting, we are giving our attention to something in a diffused way. In this mindset, we would have some trouble engaging as everything seems harder to decipher. We can just make out from this photo that it's a tree and little else. From an attention point of view, your thoughts might be wandering a lot in this state, and you might not feel very connected to the task you have to do. It's going to be quite difficult to complete the task in this **unfocused** state, and it's probably going to take you longer to finish.

Half-focused attention

Just like the automatic focus setting on a camera, this **half-focused attention** gives us more details about the tree in front of us, but there are certain areas that are still blurry and hard to make out. It's very possible to complete tasks in this state, and most of us do so on a regular basis, but we might be missing out on some details as a result. Our idea of how fun or interesting the task is may fluctuate, leading us to lose our motivation from time to time. When someone is chronically busy, they might be multitasking a lot, which can lead them to stay in this **half-focused** state of mind for many of the tasks they are undertaking.

Fully focused attention

Now we can see the tree in crystal-clear detail—we see the details on the trunk and the different branches. Generally, we get a much better idea of the whole tree. We are in a state of **fully focused attention** now. You feel focused and interested in what you're doing and are able to see the complete picture in front of you. It's easier to make decisions about what you need to do when you're in this clearer state of mind.

How to Warm Up Your Brain

When people slide from a **fully focused** to an **unfocused** state, they will typically feel like they've lost their motivation and interest in the task. How do we get ourselves *back* into a **fully focused** state?

We can use a **Brain Warm-Up**, which involves these three steps:

1. Ask yourself, "What types of activities get my brain 'in the mood' to focus?"
2. Then, try the **brain-stimulating activity** you've selected for 30–60 minutes to warm your brain up.
3. After you have completed the selected activity, dive straight into the task you've lost interest in doing, and see if this changes how your brain

feels about doing it. You might now find that your brain suddenly finds the task interesting again and feels motivated to move forward.

Warm Up to Avoid Freezing Up

Here's an example to get you started thinking about what **Brain Warm-Ups** might work for you.

A client wanted to learn time management techniques in order to write a chapter of a novel that he was struggling to complete because it wasn't feeling "fun" any more. Every time he sat down to write, he wound up distracting himself with other things, and he wasn't making any progress toward his goal. He said he felt really "frozen" and didn't know how to get his focus back.

I explained the idea of trying to do a **Brain Warm-Up** before he approached writing, and he made a list of possible **Brain Warm-Up** activities he could try:

Client's **Brain Warm-Up** list:

* Crossword puzzles.
* Go for a run.
* Play a video game.
* Look at Twitter.
* Read the news headlines.

Then, I asked him these questions about each of the items on the list:

* Is this an **unfocused/half-focused/fully focused** attention-related activity?
* Does this activity take 30–60 minutes to do?
* Will this activity increase your focus to do the larger task ahead, or just make you feel more tired?

Then, we re-edited his list with the new information that he provided:

Client's edited **Brain Warm-Up** list:

* Crossword puzzles—Fully focused—30 minutes.
* Go for a run—Fully focused—30 minutes.
* Play a video game—Fully focused—60 minutes, sometimes longer.
* Check out Twitter feed—Half-focused/Unfocused—Time varies.
* Read the news headlines—Unfocused—Time varies.

Both Twitter and news scanning were hard for him to gauge how long they were taking to do, and he admitted he often "lost many hours" to both. He felt they were both taking his attention away from writing his novel, which he already felt "bad" about not completing.

I call these types of activities **Time Sinkholes**, because it's easy to sink a lot of your time into them without receiving many brain benefits in return.

Warning: Time Sinkholes Ahead

We've all found ourselves doing things like this before. We think the activity we're choosing to do will inspire us, but instead, it just takes up all of our time and completely depletes our mental energy!

Have you ever lost a lot of time watching random videos, clicking on different Wikipedia pages, scrolling through social media feeds, or "adding to cart" things you don't intend to buy? All of these are very common **Time Sinkholes** for people. Maybe there are other **Time Sinkholes** that you find yourself frequently falling into?

It can be helpful to write down a list of your **top Time Sinkhole activities** to become more mindful of them throughout your day. If you're wondering when would be a good time to do these types of activities, check out **The Gear Shifter** tool.

For now, when choosing a potential **Brain-Warm-Up** activity, we want to avoid these types of **Time Sinkholes** as much as possible. A helpful way to remember this is:

Choose a Brain Warm-Up activity that sharpens your attention rather than blurs it.

And...

Choose a Brain Warm-Up activity that charges your mental energy rather than drains it.

When we re-edited this client's list, we were left with:

Client's re-edited **Brain Warm-Up** list:

* Crossword puzzles—Fully focused—30 minutes.
* Go for a run—Fully focused—30 minutes.
* Play a video game—Fully focused—Over an hour.

Of these three things, the safest ones to pick were crossword puzzles and going for a run, as the video game often took him longer than an hour to do. The reason for the 30–60-minute warm-up time limit is that you ideally want to have some mental energy left over for the next task ahead.

This time limit will keep you from burning up all your mental energy on the **Brain Warm-Up** task.

In other words, if you spent three hours stretching before going on a run, you'd probably feel too exhausted to complete the actual run!

Make sure to keep your Brain Warm-Up short to energize you rather than drain you.

The client decided to start with crossword puzzles as a way to warm-up his focus and attention before writing his book. After his 30 minutes of warm-up puzzles were up, he would then go straight into working on his novel afterwards. This meant he found a way to **fully focus** his attention again on writing his book, and it wasn't long before he finished writing the chapter he had been stuck on (and quite a few more).

Here are some other **Brain Warm-Up** activities that have worked for many people:

* Journaling for 30 minutes.
* Sudoku puzzles.
* Word searches.
* Writing haikus in a notebook.
* Sketching for 30 minutes.
* Coloring one detailed page in a coloring book.

Different Tasks, Different Warm-Ups

For different tasks, use different warm-ups for your brain. Ask yourself these questions: "What part of my brain will I need to use for the task ahead? Which **Brain Warm-Up** will match this particular part of my brain the best?"

If you're about to work on a financial spreadsheet, perhaps doing an easy organizational task might be a good warm-up. If you're going to work on a creative project, maybe journaling is a helpful thing to do. Try to match the **Brain Warm-Up** with the task you have to do next.

Stay Flexible Finding the Fun

When the **Brain Warm-Up** stops feeling fun for you to use, try to be flexible, and pick a new **Brain Warm-Up** instead. Keep it fresh; keep it "fun" and "interesting" for your brain to do.

When the Brain Warm-Up isn't fun for you to do anymore, simply find a new one that works again.

Once you're all warmed up, you'll be ready to mentally sprint toward your goals!

Worksheet: Write it out!

Write out 3–5 short activities you would like to do to "warm up" your brain to prepare for completing a bigger task. These activities should be 30–60 minutes long, and should engage your attention in a **fully focused** way that feels positive to you. Pick different types of **Brain Warm-Ups** for different tasks you want to do.

Brain Warm-Up Activities
(Aim for 3–5 on your list.)

Brain Warm-Up	Task this matches:
Brain Warm-Up	Task this matches:
Brain Warm-Up	Task this matches:
Brain Warm-Up	Task this matches:
Brain Warm-Up	Task this matches:
Brain Warm-Up	Task this matches:

Now write out a brief list of **Time Sinkhole** activities you tend to spend a lot of time doing that typically drain your mental energy (e.g., Twitter, scrolling social media, etc.). Then, try to avoid doing these things the next time you need to get into a **fully focused** state.

☆

Frequent **Time Sinkholes**:

. . . .

. . . .

. . . .

. . . .

. . . .

. . . .

THE GEAR SHIFTER

Do people frequently tell you that you move too fast? Do you often catch yourself rushing through things at breakneck speed? Do you continually find yourself leaping from one task to another without pausing? Have people told you that you're like a hummingbird, a busy bee, or a racing car going 100 miles per hour?

You might laugh, but these are common things I hear from clients I work with! Whether they have anxiety, ADHD, or are chronically busy from hectic schedules, there is a tendency for busy people to move *too* quickly a lot of the time.

I can relate. I've often been told that I am "too busy" and going "too fast," and I've frequently stressed myself out from getting stuck in high gear for too long. However, over the years, I've learned how to do just the opposite: To slow down deliberately.

There is a classical adage from Ancient Rome for this: "Make haste slowly." When we slow down deliberately and allow ourselves to fully engage in the task in front of us, we can finish it more thoroughly and get ourselves into a "flow" state with the task. And when we're in the flow, we lose our sense of time-related urgency. Instead, time now appears to stretch to suit our needs.

*When we consciously slow ourselves down
and complete things one task at a time,
we can find our flow again.*

At first, it can be an uncomfortable feeling for those who naturally move fast to slow down on purpose. Here's a way to remember this:

*When you're going at what you think is a "slow" speed,
you might actually just be going at a "regular" speed.*

In other words: If you're used to going 100 miles per hour down the freeway, and you cut that down by half, you're still going 50 miles per hour down the freeway.

There's a time and place for going 100 miles an hour; it just can't be all the time! Ideally, we want to be able to shift gears more smoothly, depending on what we want to accomplish. **The Gear Shifter** helps us navigate the transition of deliberately slowing down, and also helps us figure out when it's okay to deliberately speed back up again.

Shifting Gears

If you've ever driven a stick shift car, you will know that you have to press the clutch down with your foot while switching gears with your hand to get the car to go up or down a notch in speed. If you fail to do this correctly and try to wrench down the gears too hard, the car's clutch will make a terrible grinding sound and bump around a little. Sometimes you'll even smell burning rubber afterward, which will remind you to switch the gears more gently next time.

Sometimes, people who are used to being stuck in "high gear" can't always downshift gears without the clutch grinding and things getting a little bumpy, emotionally. Often, people will say that they feel "anxious" or "restless" in this state, and just can't "settle their brains down."

To start this exercise, what do the **different gears** feel like to you in your body and your brain? Take a few minutes and journal about your experience of each gear on the list.

The Different Gears

High gear: This gear can get you to your destination quickly, but you don't have as much reaction time should an obstacle suddenly block your path. While you might be **fully focused** on what you need to complete, being in high gear for a long stretch of time can be a little rough on your brain and body—not to mention on your emotional state.

Middle gear: Energy-wise, this gear feels like you're expending just enough to work at a leisurely pace. It's not as taxing as going high gear, but it also might take you a little longer to get to your destination. However, you will probably be a lot calmer when you finally arrive.

Low gear: Now you're moving fairly slowly. Low gear can be a good way to relax, let inspiration in, and take in the scenery. However, if you're working on a deadline, you might need to pick up the pace a little to make some forward progress.

When to Change Gears

To gently change gears, you can apply many of the tools we've learned previously in this chapter.

To upshift gears, you can use:

* **Brain Warm-Ups**
* **Time Buffers** (especially those that involve movement)

To downshift gears, you can use:

* **Task Desserts**
* **Time Buffers** (especially those that are more relaxing in nature)
* **Time Sinkholes**

First, ask yourself: "Where am I intending to go, mental energy-wise?"
    Here are your choices:

Low gear   Middle gear   High gear

Let's say the answer to this question is "low gear," perhaps because you have been working on a detailed work project in "high gear" for the last three hours. You're feeling mentally fried from all the concentration you've just used up and you just want to mentally unwind.
    How do you switch out of high gear? By **downshifting** gears.

Downshifting from **High gear → Low gear**

Try a **Time Sinkhole** activity.

Time Sinkhole activities blur your mental focus and attention, and should be something you do at the end of the day when you definitely don't have anything left to do task-wise, to purposely diffuse your attention to an **unfocused** state. So, if you wanted to watch random YouTube videos for an hour or two, or scroll through Twitter, now would be your chance!

Downshifting from **High gear** → **Middle gear**?

If you need to transition from high to middle gear because your day isn't quite finished yet, try using a **Task Dessert** or a **Time Buffer** activity, as both of these will glide you out of a fully focused state into a calmer mindset.

and

Task Desserts are low-level intensity tasks that feel more "fun" to do. **Time Buffers** are short breaks you take to reset your brain and body (for example: journaling, meditating, listening to music, going for a walk).

Neuroscience nugget: If you've been feeling rushed, like "there's not enough time," one way to slow down your perception of time is to take an outside **Time Buffer break** in a natural setting, looking at trees, plants, or flowers. In three different studies, participants perceived time to "slow down" when they were sitting in nature compared to when they were in more urban atmospheres, even though the lengths of time were exactly the same (Dawson and Sleek, 2018).

How to Speed Up

How do we get ourselves from **Low** to **High gear**, energy-wise? One quick way would be to try the **Brain Warm-Up** tool.

Low gear → High gear

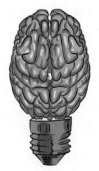

Brain Warm-Up activities stimulate your attention and focus for a short period of time. Examples of **Brain Warm-Ups** might be word puzzles, light organizational tasks, journaling, or sketching, or some other task that stimulates your brain but doesn't drain you, energy-wise.

How about **Low** to **Middle gear**? Again, when trying to get into middle gear, **Time Buffer** activities can help.

Low gear → Middle gear

In this case, since we are **going up** in gears, choose a specific **movement-based Time Buffer** that resets you by getting you to move your body. Doing light exercise, stretching, or going for a quick walk may help to stimulate your brain into a higher gear.

Grinding the Gears

Sometimes, what goes wrong for people when it comes to shifting gears is that they want to accomplish this equation:

Low gear → High gear

However, they are trying to accomplish it like this:

Low gear → Time Sinkhole → Low gear

Does this sound familiar? We've all done this one before. Using a **Time Sinkhole** activity to get out of low gear doesn't work so well. It just keeps you in low gear longer—it just grinds the gears.

A more helpful formula might be:

Low gear → Brain Warm-Up → Higher gear

Our brains need to warm-up with **attention-centering activities** before they feel ready to tackle higher-intensity tasks. It's like stretching your brain before a mental sprint!

Low Gear at Night

A few years ago, I downloaded an app of the classic game, "Settlers of Catan," which I remembered from college as being a fun game to play. My goal was to play the app around bedtime as a way to calm my brain down by deliberately downshifting gears.

In reality, what actually happened was, I became so involved in trying to beat the AI players in the game (there was one computer game player who was a seriously ruthless road builder) that I unintentionally stayed up until 2 am trying to build the longest road ever…which…never once happened. My attempt to de-stress myself had only stressed me out more, plus I wasn't getting any sleep now either (or any victory points)!

Clearly, it was not the right **Time Sinkhole** for me to fall into for relaxation purposes. Now, I tend to read books and journal at night instead, which seems to work much better for my particular brain.

What are some ways you've accidentally triggered your stress at night instead of soothed it?

Neuroscience nugget: Many people are tempted to "doomscroll 'til dawn," a term coined to define the act of scrolling through fear-inducing news headlines on our phones at night. However, the act of doom-scrolling can have negative effects on your brain, according to Dr. Pavan Madan from Community Psychiatry, who explains, "Being constantly showered with fear-inducing content can lead to a variety of anxiety issues that can cause physical and mental discomfort." Dr. Madan warns us, "Staying up late at night while doomscrolling not only encroaches in your sleep time, but also makes it harder to fall asleep" (quoted in Spector, 2020).

Try to choose *soothing* activities rather than *stressful* ones to downshift gears at night.

Consciously shift your brain into low gear with relaxing activities when it's close to bedtime.

Let's think about how we can gently transition between the different gears in a way that helps you get stuff done, while also allowing you to relax when that's what you need to do.

Worksheet: Write it out!

Using **The Gear Shifter**, write out what **low**, **middle**, and **high** gears feel like to you. Then, think of different ways to transition between the gears, using different types of activities to avoid grinding the gears.

Low gear (Write out what this feels like in your brain and body):

....

....

What activities help me shift to **Middle gear**?

....

....

Middle gear (Write out what this feels like in your brain and body):

....

....

What activities help me shift into **High gear?**

....

....

High gear (Write out what this feels like in your brain and body):

....

....

What activities help me **downshift** from **High gear** to **Low gear**?

....

....

— CHAPTER ROUND-UP —

☑ Rate tasks using **The Task Intensity Meter**.

☑ Recognize the different states of attention.

☑ Save low-intensity tasks for **Task Desserts**.

☑ Use **Brain Warm-Ups** to activate your attention.

☑ Use **Time Buffers** as a way to reset yourself.

☑ Figure out which **mental gear** to shift into.

CHAPTER 2

When You Want to Get Organized...

- ∗ The Weekly Post-It
- ∗ The Odds & Ends List
- ∗ The Time Containers
- ∗ The Color Coder
- ∗ The Stuff Station
- ∗ The Stuff Round-Up
- ∗ The Day Bookends

THE WEEKLY POST-IT

Have you ever looked at your weekly schedule ahead and felt instantly overwhelmed by everything that you had to do? Do you often feel "flooded" when you start to think about organizing all of your weekly tasks ahead?

When you have an overly busy mind or an overly busy schedule, it can sometimes be tricky to figure out what to prioritize next. The reason for this is that our prefrontal cortex (PFC), which is normally like an efficient office clerk that sorts through tasks, emotions, and decisions, can become "frozen" when too much stress is experienced all at once. Some clients describe this as feeling "flooded" or "overwhelmed" in their brains, and they can't figure out what steps to take next.

For those with ADHD, this "flooded" feeling can be even more intense, as their PFC, which would normally process and prioritize all this incoming information, may work a little differently.

> **Neuroscience nugget:** According to new neuroscience studies targeting the PFC in ADHD patients, the PFC may have weaker connectivity, which some researchers believe may be tied to dopamine irregularities in the ADHD brain. Dr. Amy Arnsten explains that the PFC requires different neurotransmitters (norepinephrine (NE) and dopamine (DA)) to work correctly: "The PFC requires an optimal level of NE and DA for proper function: either too little (as when we are drowsy or fatigued) or too much (as when we are stressed) markedly impairs PFC regulation of behavior and thought" (Arnsten, 2009).

So how do we avoid this feeling of our PFC "drowning in information" and start to swim toward calmer shores?

To-Do List Troubles

A lot of us try to tackle feeling overwhelmed by creating a to-do list. However, creating a to-do list can lead to many problems for many people, especially when they are making it from a stressed-out mental place.

Here are two common to-do list problems:

* The to-do list is way, way too long. The to-do list is packed full of little tasks, big tasks, and jumbled miscellaneous tasks all in a gigantic list that makes people feel even more "flooded" as a result.

* The list is not taking into consideration what needs to happen right now. As in, this week—not in a month, a year, etc.

The Weekly Post-It can help you avoid these potential problems while also providing you with a way to feel more positive about each task you accomplish.

How to Write Your Weekly Post-It

To begin, buy a pack of Post-Its, regular sized, in a color that catches your eye. Every Monday morning, take a few minutes to write out your **Weekly Post-It**.

Your Post-It will contain 3–5 tasks that need to be completed that particular week, filtering out other tasks that you "wish you could/should do/want to someday do," down into one simplified list.

But why use a Post-It? Sometimes, people want to use a notebook instead. The main reason for using a Post-It is that it naturally solves the problem of making a to-do list that is *way too long*. By using a Post-It, you are physically limited by the small size of the paper. When clients write in notebooks, sometimes their weekly to-do lists will stretch across dozens of pages. And that isn't setting ourselves up to reduce our brain overwhelm; it's just creating more of it.

An easy way to avoid this is to remember:

Longer to-do list = Increases stress

vs.

Shorter to-do list = Reduces stress

Also, consider that the longer you make your to-do list, the more your confidence to complete the tasks plunges as a result:

Longer to-do list = Lowers confidence to complete list

vs.

Shorter to-do list = Raises confidence to complete list

Pick Up a Pen

In addition to wanting to create endless to-do lists for themselves to tackle, many people often want to use apps for organizing tasks. Sometimes, these apps can be helpful in motivating us to get started, and if that works for you, that's great! However, in my experience, when clients have chosen to use organizational apps, they typically only use them for a week or two, and then the apps tend to get lost in a sea of other apps on their phones. In fact, sometimes searching for the "ideal" organizational app for hours just turns into a sneaky **Time Sinkhole** for many people, one that seldom leads to them actually using the app. Instead, consider using a simple Post-It and a pen. There's just something about the manual process of writing something down on paper that can really help your brain remember things.

Neuroscience nugget: In a neuroscience study done at the University of Tokyo, researchers discovered that writing by hand on a physical sheet of paper improved people's processing of information compared to when they wrote on a digital tablet. Researchers found that writing by hand causes us to use different parts of our brain, including complex regions related to spatial reasoning, and this may form a stronger brain association overall that assists our memory. As Professor K.L. Sakai explains: "Actually, paper is more advanced and useful compared to electronic documents because paper contains more one-of-a-kind information for stronger memory recall" (Umejima *et al.*, 2021).

In other words, writing something down with a pen on paper can help boost your brain's retention of that information. Additionally, when you cross something off your **Weekly Post-It,** you can also get a little dopamine boost because now your brain *feels* like it's completed the task.

Crossing an item off your list allows you to fully connect with your success.

Rules for your **Weekly Post-It:**

* **Pick a color of Post-It that gets your attention.** Try to avoid white or pastel colors, as they might not grab your visual attention as easily.
* **Write down 3–5 things you have to do this week only.** Try to avoid writing more than 5 things. Ideally, everything should fit neatly in a way that you can read it clearly on one single sticky note. This is an easy way for you to get to the core of what you actually need to do, instead of things you "think you should/wish you could" do.
* **Put up your Weekly Post-It somewhere you will actually see it every day.** Most people place their **Weekly Post-It** near their computer or on a surface that they visually notice every day, like on their bathroom mirror or their refrigerator.
* **As you complete a task on your Weekly Post-It, cross it off!** This is an important piece of the process because you are taking a moment to acknowledge that a task is finally done. You've completed it. You did what you set out to do.
* **Do not add any more items to your list until the following Monday morning.** When we get on a roll with completing things, we sometimes want to move ahead too quickly, and this can overwhelm us all over again. Stick to completing 3–5 things a week consistently instead.
* When you're done with all the tasks, throw **The Weekly Post-It** away triumphantly!

For Unfinished Tasks...

For any items you were unable to complete that week, carry them over to the new **Weekly Post-It**. For example, if you were unable to finish a work progress report on Friday, carry it over to the next week's list on Monday.

Old Weekly Post-It:

New Weekly Post-It:

Because you didn't have a chance to complete the work progress report last week, it now moves to the top of the new **Weekly Post-It**. After that, two new tasks have been added underneath. This is an easy way we can keep our to-do list from growing way too long.

Motivational Micro-Thoughts

Every time you complete something on your list, build in some soothing self-talk to help motivate yourself. These are gentle little self-talk phrases that can ease you into a positive place in a way that your brain won't instantly reject. I call these phrases **micro-thoughts**.

Micro-thoughts are tiny thoughts that our brains will typically believe because they don't make us feel like we're making a big scary leap over to extreme positivity. Instead, they feel like tiny steps in a positive direction that feel more manageable for us to take. We will learn to practice more of them in future chapters (see: **The Wall Crusher, The Word Selector**), as they can help you increase your sense of resiliency.

For now, here are a few **Weekly Post-It micro-thoughts** to begin to use with **The Weekly Post-It:**

"I completed what I set out to do and I am learning to enjoy this feeling."

"It is such a relief to cross this item off my list!"

"I feel a little better each time I complete something on my list."

"Every completed item is a small success that I am going to let myself enjoy for a few minutes."

Now let's practice writing out our **Weekly Post-It** so that we can triumphantly cross items off as we soon as we complete them.

Worksheet: Write it out!

Write down 3–5 things that need to get done this week. Leave off extraneous items that you "should/wish you could/might want to do." Focus on simplifying your list down. After you do each item on your list, cross it off and let yourself feel proud!

My Weekly Post-it Note:

THE ODDS & ENDS LIST

You might now be wondering, "But where am I supposed to put all the little tasks you told me I couldn't put on my **Weekly Post-It**?"

I call these types of miscellaneous tasks **Odds & Ends** and they go on a separate list called: **The Odds & Ends List**. Remember, these aren't "have to complete these items this week" types of tasks—those would go directly on your **Weekly Post-It**. Instead, these are "I should really complete these at some…vague…point…in the future" kinds of everyday tasks. For bigger long-term goals, you can use **The Goal Splicer** tool in the next chapter.

Your **Odds & Ends List** can be in a notebook, on an excel spreadsheet, or whatever feels the most comfortable to you. These are tasks that don't have a pressing deadline, but they're still tasks that are nagging at your brain a lot during the week.

Here are some examples of what clients put on their **Odds & Ends List**:

* Organize office.
* Order new filing cabinet.
* Hang guitar on the wall somewhere that is easy to access.
* Pay a parking ticket that isn't due for a month.
* Add up income from business for the last few months.

Because you might not have a defined deadline for these types of tasks, you might not be moving forward on any of these things, and this can cause us to think a lot of negative self-talk such as, "I still haven't finished that task" or "This task feels so bad to even look at doing!"

As a result, just thinking about these tasks stresses you out and makes you want to push them further down on your to-do list. Unfortunately, this only makes your brain want to "ping" you about these tasks even more!

Odds & Ends List Rules

Here are a few rules for approaching these miscellaneous tasks each week:

* Each week, after you complete your **Weekly Post-It**, update your **Odds & Ends List**. This way, you will already know what the essential tasks are before you start writing the non-essential tasks down. Try to keep your **Odds & Ends List** down to one page. It can be longer than your **Weekly Post-It**, but not *so* long that it makes you feel like you want to avoid looking at it altogether.
* Every week on Sunday, make sure you have done at least *one item* on your **Odds & Ends List**.
* Do not add a new item to your **Odds & Ends List** until you have crossed one old item off.

You can remember this equation:

$$\textit{1 Odds \& Ends task on = 1 Odds \& Ends task off}$$

It's not uncommon for me to ask a client how long an item has been on their list and for them to answer, "Oh, I don't know, six months or so." That's six months of daily mental reminders for that one small task, which is costing you a lot of mental energy overall. Wouldn't it be great to get some relief from those brain-nagging reminders by just tackling your one odd task at a time?

Every time you clear out a miscellaneous item from your **Odds & Ends List**, tell yourself a **motivational micro-thought:**

"I no longer have to worry about this miscellaneous task any more. I can leave room to think about other things now."

"I am getting better at completing small tasks each week."

"Every time I complete a small task, it makes completing bigger tasks easier to do."

"Small steps add up."

Small steps really do add up—trust that by doing a little each week, you will get you where you need to go.

Worksheet: Write it out!

After writing down your 3–5 essential tasks on your **Weekly Post-It**, put all the leftover miscellaneous tasks on the list below. Then, circle one small task on your **Odds & Ends List** to complete by the end of the week:

1. . . . .

2. . . . .

3. . . . .

4. . . . .

5. . . . .

6. . . . .

7. . . . .

8. . . . .

9. . . . .

10. . . . .

When you've finished your small miscellaneous task, remember to cross it off and give yourself some self-praise!

THE TIME CONTAINERS

One way to start organizing your time more effectively is to use a tool called **The Time Containers**. This is a way of seeing your time as "compartmentalized," which means that you are only focusing on one set of tasks at a time and you are plugging these **Time Containers** into your calendar as consistent blocks of time in specific colors each week.

To begin with, take a few seconds to visualize a few different sized containers:

Now, mentally put a label on each container based on things you want to do consistently each week. For example, your **Time Container** labels might be labelled: "Work tasks," "Self-care," "Creative projects."

Then, on your weekly calendar, begin to plug the **Time Containers** into their designated time slots:

Monday	Tuesday	Wednesday
9–5 Work tasks	9–5 Work tasks	9–5 Work tasks
7–9 Self-care	7–8 Household tasks	7–9 Creative projects

Now, change the color of each **Time Container** to a different color on your calendar so you can see them clearly. Let's start with the largest container, "Work tasks," and make that **green** for now, and let's begin with Monday:

Monday
9–5 Work tasks (Green section)
7–9 Self-care

Within the **green "Work tasks" section** from 9–5 on Monday you can now break down your work tasks inside that **Time Container** by dividing up the container into smaller hour chunks, keeping all of it green. Now, when we see the **green Time Container** on Monday, it might look something like this:

Monday: Work tasks (Green section)
9–10 Answer work emails
10–12 Meetings
1–3 Write report
3–5 Misc. work projects

The next step is to rate each of your "Work tasks" with a **task intensity level code** by adding a ranking of **Low** (L), **Mid** (M), or **High** (H) intensity afterwards.

Monday: Work tasks (Green section)
9–10 Answer work emails (L)
10–12 Meetings (H)
1–3 Write report (H)
3–5 Misc. work projects (M)

Listing the **task intensity codes** will help you figure out when you need to take **Time Buffer breaks**, as well as if you want to move tasks around to better suit your energy levels. For instance, maybe you want to swap out "Misc. work projects" with "Write report" because that feels easier for you to do after lunch? Great! That means you're getting more in tune with doing tasks based on the amount of mental and physical energy you have to complete them, and you're adjusting it accordingly on a regular basis that is custom-tailored to you.

Now that we've completed the **green "Work tasks" section**, the next section on this sample Monday list is a smaller time container called **"Self-care,"** which we can add in **blue**, and might look something like this:

Monday: Self-care (Blue section)
7–9 Meditation, coloring, journaling

For **Time Containers** with tasks inside that don't have to be broken down hourly, you can simply write out a list of related activities to choose from. This now gives you activities to pick from that are related to "Self-care" and that you can do every Monday during that time slot. Having choices keeps things "interesting" for your brain, which increases your chances of completing this **Time Container** consistently.

Give Yourself a Few Choices

When we get too "rigid" and "strict" with our scheduling, it can sometimes lead us to procrastinate. For example, on Monday, if you've scheduled a **Time Container** called "Jogging" after work, but you frequently find that you are too tired to go for a jog, you might start to mentally ignore this section of your calendar each week.

Instead, you could re-label this more generally as "Exercise," and within it, give yourself a bunch of different options to choose from that cover different levels of energy for you (for example: "Exercise: Running, walking, stretching, lifting small weights").

You can do this with other **Time Containers** too, such as "Creative projects" (for example: "Drawing, guitar, knitting") or "Hobbies" (for example: "Baking, photography, gardening").

Now on days when you're not up for something like going for a jog or working on your garden, you have given yourself many other options in those categories to pick from instead.

Get Honest with Yourself About Time

When we're in a stressed-out mindset, there is a tendency to underestimate how much time something will take to complete. In other words, we just don't give ourselves enough time to realistically get something done.

Sometimes, clients will write out a time container like "9–10 Answer work emails" only to find that this task actually took two hours to complete instead of one. Or they will write something like: "5–5:30 Write report" when in reality they spent three hours writing the report instead of 30 minutes.

Are you frequently way off with your **time estimates** of how long something will actually take you to do?

Try this for one week: Keep track of how long tasks actually take you to complete. Collect useful data that will help you plan things more realistically in the future. In other words, get really honest with yourself about how long things are taking you to do.

Use the example below to create a chart for yourself. At the end of the week, compare the difference between your time estimates vs. reality. Here's a sample chart:

Time estimates vs. reality

Monday		
My estimate	**In reality**	**Time difference**
9–10 Work emails	9–11 Work emails	1 hour
1–2 Finish researching project	1–3 Finish meeting notes	1 hour
5–5:30 Write report	5–8 Write report	2.5 hours
6–7 Grocery store	6–7:30 Grocery store	30 minutes

After seeing all of the data in front of you, you may begin to understand why you frequently feel like you're running out of time each week. It's quite possible that you just aren't giving yourself time to do everything on your schedule on a regular basis.

It's helpful to remember:

Schedule more time than you need to complete things, not less.

Set yourself up for success by giving yourself more than enough time to get things done.

The "Fill Up the Empty Hour" Problem

When we see an open slot on our calendar, many of us have a knee-jerk reaction to "fill up the empty hour" by instantly plugging in something for ourselves to do. We momentarily forget that we have a limited amount of energy to spend each day, and we need to give ourselves adequate **Time Buffer breaks** to reset ourselves. It can be helpful to remind yourself:

Filling up every free slot on your calendar = Mental exhaustion

When you feel the need to plug in too many activities in your calendar without gaps of time in between, ask yourself, "Why am I trying to over-stack my time each day? Why am I not allowing myself to have enough downtime in between tasks to rest my brain and body?"

You deserve regular time in your schedule to relax and unwind. Your brain and body will thank you!

Time Boundaries

Keeping your **Time Containers** consistent can strengthen your sense of **time boundaries**.

When we give our brains endless time to do tasks during a day, it's difficult to conceptualize how much time a task will actually take and how much mental energy we're going to need for the task. When we give ourselves clear start and end times for each set of tasks, it's easier for us to gauge how much energy we're going to need to complete them.

Neuroscience nugget: In a study done at Tel Aviv University, participants had to take a very long test that included 2400 tasks, divided up into different blocks of time. One group was told how many tasks they would have to complete during how many different blocks of time, while the other group was given no information on time or number of tasks. The first group that knew how many tasks there were going to be and how long the blocks of time would last performed faster and more accurately than the group that had no information (Katzir, Emanuel, and Liberman, 2020).

By making your perception of time more precise in relation to a task, you can start to use your mental energy more effectively to complete tasks within those time parameters.

Beware of the Multitasking Tornado

When we let our **time boundaries** become too "loosey-goosey," there's a tendency to let multitasking creep back in, and as a result, our attention can sometimes become unfocused and disengaged.

When I work with **Chronically Busy Clients** who have a lot of energy, a lot of responsibilities, and a lot of projects to manage, I've noticed that they will frequently multitask themselves into a state of mental and emotional burn-out. I call this the **"Multitasking Tornado,"** and it tends to whisk away people who take on too many tasks at once!

Sometimes this habit of chronic multitasking comes from a feeling like you have to "people-please" a lot of the time. Often, in our attempts to accommodate other's needs, it can be very easy to overlook our own.

For instance, if a friend calls you at the very last minute on a very busy work day and asks you to go to lunch, and you're more worried about your friend's schedule than your own, you'll probably go to lunch anyway, and then your tasks will pile up afterward. This will most likely cause you to feel really stressed out for the rest of the day.

However, if you're mindful of your own mental energy and your **Time Containers,** when a friend asks you to drop everything, you can think, "Do I want to move this whole set of tasks to another day to accommodate this request right now? Or should I ask my friend if we can meet during a different slot of time that both of us have free instead?"

When we make frequent knee-jerk decisions to accommodate other people's schedules, it takes a toll on our stress levels and emotional states. This is one way the multitasking tornado can sneak up on us and easily derail our plans for the day, especially if we're doing this a lot throughout the week...for multiple people with multiple last-minute requests.

Instead, think of honoring your own **time boundaries** a little more each week. You don't have to be too rigid about it; you can adjust it as you go. If your friend is only in town for the day, maybe you decide it's worth it to move your schedule around. But if your friend lives nearby and has plenty of free time, maybe finding a more optimal time for both of you is the way to go.

Simplify Your Schedule

Practice keeping these simple rules in mind when scheduling your week:

* Take things one **Time Container** at a time.
* Make sure you are scheduling yourself *more* than enough time for tasks you need to do based on **realistic time estimates**.

* Keep your **Time Containers** the same times and on the same days each week as much as possible.
* Within your **Time Containers,** rate the designated tasks by intensity and arrange them in a way that feels balanced to you.
* For "Hobbies," "Exercise," and "Self-care" **Time Containers,** give yourself a few options of related activities to choose from within the set time frame each week.
* Avoid over-stacking your **Time Containers.** Give yourself some space to reset in between things.

By establishing healthier **time boundaries,** you will now start to dodge many multitasking tornados that want to whisk you away. You'll achieve more overall by directing your focus more deliberately each week, and you might even find that you now have more time to relax as well.

In fact, why not make "Relaxation" a consistent **Time Container,** too?

Worksheet: Color it out!

Using the illustration below, label out your different **Time Containers** with different sets of tasks you would like to schedule each week (e.g., "Work tasks," "Creative projects," "Self-care," "Exercise," etc.). Then, color each one with a specific color you will associate with those tasks. For example, "Work tasks" = green, "Creative projects" = orange, "Self-care" = purple.

After you've labeled and colored your **Time Containers**, start plugging them into your weekly calendar as consistent color blocks of time.

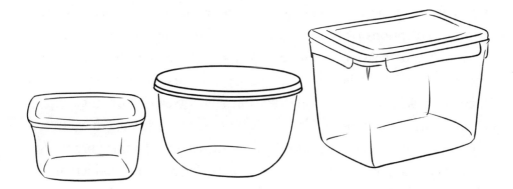

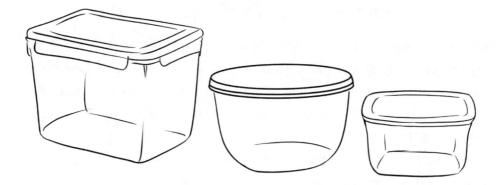

Visit www.timemanagementtoolkit.com to view sample weekly **Time Container** schedules and templates.

THE COLOR CODER

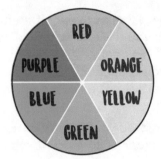

In the field of consumer psychology, psychologists study how colors affect people's perceptions of products. Reds tend to make us feel things like "strength" and "passion," blues can symbolize "trustworthiness," greens denote "growth," and yellows and oranges can make us feel "happy" and "energetic." What color a brand picks for their logo can have a huge impact on how much money they make and what type of consumers they attract.

Clearly, colors have a powerful psychological effect on our brains. So, how can we train our brains to improve our efficiency and productivity by utilizing the concept of **color coding** in everyday life?

"Absent-Minded Professor" Mode

In my work with adult clients who have ADHD, I often hear about how they lose everyday objects like keys and phones on a daily basis. One client described this as "going into absent-minded professor mode," where she would become so lost in thought throughout the day that she would often misplace her keys.

Around the same time, three other clients told me they were experiencing similar problems misplacing their phones daily.

While becoming forgetful with small, everyday objects can be a common issue for those with ADHD, I have also heard this from clients who are chronically busy or distracted by multiple responsibilities as well. Parents of small children (especially those who are chronically sleep-deprived) can also be susceptible to misplacing commonly used objects. In my case, when my kids were babies who never seemed to sleep, I frequently asked people where my sunglasses were…when they were on top of my head.

After trying other methods that weren't working to solve the problem of misplaced phones, glasses, and keys, I finally stumbled on one that actually worked for many people. And the solution involved using **color**.

For the client who was misplacing her keys a lot, I explained how I used to have this same problem with my sunglasses, until I bought a small tray to put them in, which happened to be **red**. I explained that, somehow, putting my sunglasses in a red tray helped me remember to **stop** and put them there each time I came in the door. You can remember this trick like this:

Use the color red to tell your brain to stop and do something.

In between sessions, the client found a small red bowl and tried out putting her keys in it every day of the week. Because of our discussion, she had already formed the brain association:

Red = Keys

And it worked! She stopped losing her keys because she remembered to use the red bowl every day.

She had made this mental equation:

What colors might work to make you stop and remember something?

Color Code Your Phone

Around the same time, I had a few clients who were struggling to put their phones away when it was time to work. Instead, they would automatically pick up their phones and quickly go into **Time Sinkholes**, procrastinating their work-related tasks. One client confessed, "If I could just have someone physically take my phone away for a few hours, I might actually get some work done!"

I suggested leaving the phone on the charger in a separate room for a scheduled **phone time-out** each day, and this really helped many clients get their focus back.

However, I still had one client for whom this strategy wasn't working. First of all, he lived in a small space, so it was hard to find somewhere he couldn't see his phone. Because he could still easily access it, he would often absent-mindedly pick it up and go straight into a **Time Sinkhole** activity before he could catch himself. He was in his last semester of graduate school and said he was spending "way too much time on his phone" and "not enough time studying."

We needed to form a better brain association for a **phone time-out** as just leaving it on a charger wasn't enough. I told him about how powerful the color red can be for making our brains "stop." I asked him to think if there was something red he could put his phone on? I was hoping this might create the brain association:

Red = Phone time-out

Between sessions, he found an old textbook with a bright red cover. When it was time for him to study, he put the phone on top of the red textbook.

Something clicked! He no longer haphazardly picked up his phone on autopilot when it was time to study. The connection had been made:

Phone on red book = Phone time-out

"What worked?" I asked him.

He said, "The color red. And also, I associate that book with a class I don't ever want to take again. So, when I see the red and the textbook together, I think: 'I should really start studying!'"

Using **The Color Coder**

Take a second to think about colors and what emotions or associations they bring up for you.

What are some colors that make you feel happy? What colors make you stop and think? What colors make you feel calm and relaxed? What colors make you feel more focused?

And then think, "How can I use these **pre-existing color associations** to my advantage when setting up new brain associations with doing tasks?"

Here are some ideas from clients who enjoyed playing around with **The Color Coder:**

* "I use different colors to block off certain tasks on my calendar in certain colors. I put work tasks in blue. **Time Buffer** activities are in green. Social activities are in orange. This helps me keep them separate mentally."
* "I use a polka dot dish to keep my phone in at night so I won't forget where my phone is. It also helps remind me to take a break from my phone."
* "I use different color notebooks to journal about different things: One is green and one is bright orange. Seeing different brightly colored journals makes me feel more motivated to write in each of them every day."
* "I keep bills that need to be paid in a red tray by the door so I remember to pay them. I keep mail that needs to be mailed in a green tray so I remember to take it with me."
* "I write different goals down for the week in different colors. My main goals are red, my creative goals are green, and my self-care goals are purple. Every week, I use the same colors, so that when I flip through the pages, it's easy to see the progress in each category."

After reading all these different and creative approaches, how can you **color code** things to your brain's advantage?

Worksheet: Write it out!

Answer the following questions about colors. Then, think of certain tasks or habits where you can utilize **color coding** as a way to help your brain feel more motivated!

What color makes you "stop"?

. . . .

. . . .

What color do you associate with "relaxing" or "self-care"?

. . . .

. . . .

What color do you associate with "focus" or "energy"?

. . . .

. . . .

Now, think of some ways you can use these colors to develop new mental habits (e.g., "I can put my phone in a red dish so I don't lose it," or, "I can color-code my calendar self-care activities in green"):

1.. . . . .

. . . .

. . . .

. . . .

. . . .

. . . .

☆

2. . . . .
. . . .
. . . .
. . . .
. . . .
. . . .
. . . .

3. . . . .
. . . .
. . . .
. . . .
. . . .
. . . .
. . . .

☆

THE STUFF STATION

The stuff we own can create a lot of time-related stress in our daily lives. How can this be true? We love our stuff so much! And yet, chronically accumulating *too* much stuff may be causing you to have to make hundreds (if not thousands) of daily decisions that are costing you a lot of valuable time each day.

In our Western society, we have a strange relationship with stuff. Advertisements, social media, and articles constantly tell us we need stuff. When we feel anxious, stressed, or depressed, we buy stuff. When we're feeling bored, we buy even more stuff. In this way, we tend to accumulate *a lot* of stuff! Since everything these days is "instantly" sent to our homes, all it takes is a click of a button and more stuff is quickly rushed to our doorstep.

Convenience-wise, this is great. However, organizationally, this may not be working out so well in your home.

The dopamine surge we experience in our brains when we "impulse buy" is short-lived compared to the overwhelm and stress we feel when we have to unpack, sort through, and organize all the stuff we just purchased, leading us to feel a sense of **"stuff exhaustion"** from **"decision fatigue."** Decision fatigue is the concept that having to make many tiny decisions each day can add up to big feelings of mental exhaustion.

Neuroscience nugget: Decision fatigue, according to writer John Tierney, is "different from ordinary physical fatigue—you're not consciously aware of being tired—but you're low on mental energy. The more choices you make throughout the day, the harder each one becomes for your brain." Researchers tested this theory by giving random mall shoppers a simple arithmetic test. What they found was, the shoppers who had purchased the most things beforehand did worse overall on the test compared to the shoppers who hadn't purchased anything. The researchers hypothesized this result was from decision fatigue from making shopping choices all day (Tierney, 2011).

So, how do we minimize our decisions related to stuff, so that we can feel more mentally energized each day?

Short-Term vs. Long-Term Stuff

One way to change how you approach your relationship to stuff is to start to see stuff from a **long-term** rather than a **short-term** perspective.

For example, when you buy something, you have to spend time finding a place to put it and then you have to spend time taking care of it. All of our things require different levels of upkeep to maintain them.

You can remember the equation like this:

Less stuff = Fewer future decisions to make

More stuff = More future decisions to make

More decisions to make = More mental fatigue

When people have ADHD, chronic anxiety, or are overwhelmed by their busy schedules, they might lean towards **short-term stuff solutions** rather than **long-term stuff solutions**. Impulse buying is sometimes how people try to deal with the stress they're feeling. But instead of feeling relief from all the stress, we sometimes just create more of it by giving ourselves too much stuff to manage.

> **Neuroscience nugget:** According to a study done by researchers that tracked spending and financial decisions across a group of participants: "The ADHD and Adult-only ADHD groups reported significantly more impulsive buying, used more often an avoidant or spontaneous decision style and less often saved money compared to the No ADHD group." Researchers concluded that adults with ADHD tended to use "spontaneous financial decision making" which was "disadvantageous" in the long run toward financial goals (Bangma *et al.*, 2020).

In most cases, you are seeking the feeling rather than the thing. More importantly, you are seeking connecting to the feeling most of all. And, in some cases, you might not need the stuff to just start practicing the feeling you want to feel. You might want to ask yourself, "What are some other ways I can connect with the feelings I want to feel on a regular basis?"

Personify Your Stuff

If you haven't been actively practicing seeing your stuff from a **long-term perspective**, it can be easy to disregard a sweater lying in the middle of the floor. However, if you practice seeing your stuff as something you want to have a **long-term relationship** with, you might now see the sweater on the floor and think, "Aw, poor sweater, I better pick it up and put it away!"

Now it's easy to think of where the **Stuff Station** is for the sweater—it's most likely on a hanger in your closet, where it can now live happily, instead of getting sadly stepped on.

By seeing our stuff through the eyes of appreciation more, we can learn to treat our stuff more respectfully over time. When we practice frequent feelings of appreciation for our stuff, we're actually learning to appreciate ourselves more often as a result. In other words, it causes a ripple of appreciation that happily affects other areas of our lives.

A Home for Your Stuff

To use **The Stuff Station,** here are **three questions** to ask yourself before you purchase something:

* "Does this provide a clear solution for a problem I have right now?"
* "Where specifically will I store this stuff in my house? Where will it live permanently?"
* "How often will I use this after I purchase it?"

If you can provide logical answers to all three questions, then move forward with considering whether or not you want to buy it. If you can't think of the answers, maybe hold off on a day or two before you make the purchase.

Group Things Together

As you start to consider more where to house items, it can be helpful to group similar things together. Instead of just remembering that scissors are supposed to live in the desk drawer, we could instead re-label this scissors station: **Office Supplies Station**. Everything related to office supplies—staplers, tape, markers, notepads—now lives in the same office supplies drawer together. This makes it even easier to remember where all these things should be stored.

You don't have to go on a massive organizational whirlwind throughout your house to make this idea work for you. Start *small*. When you buy a new thing, think of where its **Stuff Station** will be permanently in your house. Then, as you find stuff that relates to that new item, simply store the similar stuff together in one place.

It's a new mental habit that you can form one **Stuff Station** at a time.

Worksheet: Write it out!

What are some objects you frequently misplace or lose? Where could **The Stuff Station** for these particular items reside now permanently in your home? Pick a few items you tend to lose and write out a **Stuff Station** for each one.

Item I tend to lose or forget about:

. . . .

. . . .

New **Stuff Station**:

. . . .

. . . .

Item I tend to lose or forget about:

. . . .

. . . .

New **Stuff Station**:

. . . .

. . . .

Item I tend to lose or forget about:

. . . .

. . . .

New **Stuff Station**:

. . . .

. . . .

THE STUFF ROUND-UP

When we're chronically busy, our rooms can start to reflect the chaos. When we're lost in our thoughts, it can be altogether too easy to leave misplaced items haphazardly scattered all over our home throughout the day. You can think of it like this:

Higher level of internal distraction = Greater chance of environmental chaos

I don't know about you, but in my house, coffee mugs seem to spawn all over the place especially when I'm mentally distracted by multiple projects. By the end of a busy day, it's not unusual for me to collect at least five to six cups in different rooms during my daily **Stuff Round-Up**.

Maybe it's clothes, bags, or paperwork that spawns everywhere across multiple surfaces when you're busy or distracted? Keep the stuff-spawning in check by training your brain to do a nightly **Round-Up**. It only takes a few minutes each day, and it's an easy way to keep things in order without expending too much energy overall.

You might start to form this mental equation:

Easy Nighttime Ritual

Stuff Round-Up steps:

* Before you allow yourself to get into bed, make sure you have completed one **Stuff Round-Up** as part of your nightly routine.
* Do a scan around your home before bedtime, picking up any leftover cups, papers, and items on the floor, and put them away in their specific **Stuff Station** (see: **The Stuff Station**). The whole process shouldn't take more than 20 minutes. This is just a quick round-up of items, not a heavy-duty cleaning or organizing.

In short cleaning increments each night, you can start to change your association with organizing your home in a more positive way.

Frustrated Cleaning Blitz

Often, clients tell me that they will wait to clean and organize until they're really frustrated with the mess around them.

"I can only do a frustrated cleaning blitz when I'm mad," one busy client confessed, "it's how I've always associated cleaning and organizing. I wait until I'm so frustrated that I can't take the mess anymore!"

Many people approach cleaning this way. Sometimes, doing a deep cleaning and organizing can be a productive way to channel intense emotions like feeling frustrated or upset. However, it's important to be aware of the associations you're now forming for yourself. You might accidentally be programming your brain with this statement: "I can only clean when I'm feeling mad or frustrated."

Your brain might now see it like this:

Cleaning = Stress

If this is the accidental brain equation you have formed, you can start to shift it by thinking a gentle thought like, "I have taught myself to do deep cleaning as a way to channel intense emotions. However, I can do a light **Stuff Round-Up** each night from a calmer, everyday mindset."

You could also look at it like this:

Deep cleaning – High-intensity

Organizing one area of house – Mid-intensity

Nightly **Stuff Round-Up** – Low-intensity

In other words, a **low-intensity** night-time **Stuff Round-Up** is *way* easier to do consistently than even one **high-intensity** frustrated deep cleaning blitz.

Motivational Micro-Thoughts

Give yourself praise and encouragement whenever you complete your **Stuff Round-Up**. Here are some examples:

"I am forming new habits that are going to help me stay organized."

"I did a great job putting everything away tonight."

"Whenever I remember to put stuff away at night, I am setting myself up for an easier morning."

"I can really rest now knowing that I've put everything away for the night."

The more self-praise you give yourself for rounding up your stuff each night, the more the habit will stick. By doing things in one nightly **Stuff Round-Up**, you are mentally clearing the decks for the next day's tasks ahead.

Worksheet: Write it out!

Take some time to fill out the worksheet below and see if it helps you to remember to incorporate a **Stuff Round-Up** in your daily routine.

What are the most frequent objects I tend to leave scattered around my home? List them out below:

. . . .

. . . .

. . . .

. . . .

Write out a plan for doing a daily **Stuff Round-Up** for the objects you listed above (for example: Object: Cups, Stuff Round-Up Plan: Every night at 9 pm I will collect all the cups in every room and put them in the kitchen).

Object	Stuff Round-Up Plan

THE DAY BOOKENDS

When we wake up in the morning, we're sometimes hit with very anti-motivating thoughts. Before we've gotten out of bed, we might already be fighting a stream of negative thoughts such as, "I don't want to do that thing I have to do!" or "I will never get it all done!" Thoughts such as these can lead to a feeling of dread about the upcoming day.

And dread is the exact opposite of feeling motivated! So how can we catch ourselves before we slip into the morning dread quicksand, and get ourselves more excited to face the day?

One thing that helps is to have a pre-planned morning practice that helps your brain ramp up for your day and a nightly ritual that helps you ease back into rest mode.

You might visualize it like this:

Morning

Rest → Work

Evening

Work → Rest

(Goal: Smoother, gentler transitions)

Whether you are anxious, have ADHD, or feel frequently stressed-out, establishing daily routines can help you remember to make self-care more of a priority in your schedule.

> **Neuroscience nugget:** Steffanie Wilk and Nancy Rothbard from the Wharton School of the University of Pennsylvania studied how the morning moods of employees affected their performance and moods throughout the day. They found that employees who started the day off in a positive mood perceived their work and interactions that day from a more positive mental framework, and their overall performance improved as a result. Conversely, when employees started the day from a negative mindset, Wilk reported that "employees could get into these negative spirals where they started the day in a bad mood and just got worse over the course of the day" (Rothbard and Wilk, 2011).

In other words, taking a few minutes to start the day out from a calmer mindset just might shift the whole flow of your day.

Bookend Your Day

Think of the tasks ahead of you as books between two self-care practice bookends, **Morning** and **Night**. You can't open the books to start your work until you've passed the **Morning Bookend**. And you can't close out the night without the **Night Bookend**.

You can use some of the tools we've already established in the previous chapters, or some of the new tools suggested here. Try to pick self-care activities that will help you transition between rest and work modes more smoothly.

The following is an example of how to structure your **Day Bookends** that will allow you to start and finish your day while keeping you calm.

The Morning Bookend

Step 1: The Negativity Neutralizer

As you wake up, try to neutralize negative thoughts as they appear. These are those "morning dread" types of thoughts that sometimes flood our minds, like, "I'll never get it all done!" or "I hate all the things I have to do!" As you think these types of thoughts, catch the thoughts and stop them, with a large mental net called **The Negativity Neutralizer.**

After you hear yourself think these negative morning thoughts, catch them in **The Negativity Neutralizer net,** and add the thought: "That's a really harsh thought I'm thinking." Labeling the thoughts as "harsh" will pull you out of the thought, and it will allow you to see the thoughts as an observer. Separating your thoughts away from yourself and looking at them from a distance can help you start to feel empowered to change them. This is called developing a **mindful awareness** of your thought patterns.

It's helpful to remember:

Negative thoughts = Negative emotions

And

Positive thoughts = Positive emotions

Sometimes, first thing in the morning, we just can't get to a positive place with our thoughts. If this is true for you, try to *neutralize* your negative thoughts instead. Here's one way to remember this:

Neutralizing negative thoughts = Neutral feelings

And...

Neutral feelings tend to feel better than negative feelings

We can neutralize our thoughts by mindfully observing and labeling them as they appear. Then, it becomes easier to add in some positive thoughts to replace them, instead of getting swept away by a negative thought tidal wave.

But why, some people ask, does it feel so hard to think positive thoughts in the morning? This is because of a **cortisol awakening response** that happens to people who are feeling chronically stressed-out or anxious. It's a spike of the stress hormone cortisol flooding our brains just as our bodies are waking up—and frankly, it doesn't help us face the day at all!

Neuroscience nugget: According to Dr. Carlos Contreras and Dr. Ana Guitérrez-Garcia, we may still have the cortisol awakening response from primitive cave days: "The diurnal secretion of cortisol occurs near the time of awakening (i.e., after a period of rest or sleeping) and persists for several hours in the absence of any current stressful situation. The CAR (cortisol awakening response) seems to represent an ancient adaptive-allostatic feature that prepares an individual to face eventualities that are forthcoming during the day" (Contreras and Gutiérrez-Garcia, 2018, p.29).

This morning cortisol secretion that once helped us survive predator attacks doesn't really help our brains handle non-life-or-death tasks now, such as getting to work, packing up the kids for school, etc. It only makes us feel *more* stressed out before we've even started. Practice bypassing this **morning cortisol spike** by catching those negative thoughts and replacing them with kinder, neutralizing thoughts to ease into your day.

Here are some morning **micro-thoughts** to try out:

"I'm just waking up now and I'm taking things one thing at a time."

"I can handle any problems after I've had a chance to ease into the day."

"I'm going to take a few minutes to do some deep breathing and relax into the morning."

"I am handling things one task at a time."

"I can move at a pace that allows me to stay calm instead of rushing around."

Step 2: Square Breathing

If cortisol has been released, the fastest way to reset your brain is to take a few, long, deliberate deep breaths. One way to do this is called **Square Breathing**. It's easy to remember to do, and it only takes a few minutes of your time.

During **Square Breathing**, you inhale for four seconds, hold for four seconds, exhale for four seconds, and hold again for four seconds:

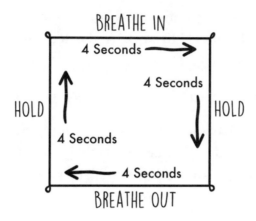

The more you practice **Square Breathing**, the more you'll remember to do it. After a while, it will come naturally to you, and you'll remember to use it every time you feel the stress rise.

Step 3: Scan Your **Weekly Post-It List**

After you've done some deep breathing and neutralized your negative thoughts, have a quick look at your **Weekly Post-It**. Take a moment to scan it, and to see if there's anything you can triumphantly cross off! If not, set your focus on which task on your list you want to take on next.

Step 4: Task Organization

Before you start anything, think about the tasks ahead of you for a few minutes. Using **The Time Containers** and **The Task Intensity Meter**, block out your **Time Containers**, order your tasks by intensity level, and add in **Time Buffer breaks** to de-stress in between **Time Containers.** This will set you up to accomplish things in a more efficient (and calmer) way.

Step 5: Brain Warm-Up

Now that you've also probably done all the morning maintenance stuff I haven't included as part of this example, like brushing your teeth, getting dressed, eating breakfast, etc., it's time to pick a **Brain Warm-Up** activity to get your brain "in the mood" to work. And then, you're off and running!

Don't Jump-Start Your Day with Stress

When my kids were babies, I would often fly into the mornings in what I'd call "firefighter mode." The alarm would go off, or a baby would be crying, and I'd jump out of bed like a firefighter having to put out a fire. Talk about a tough way to wake up!

This did not bode well for my daily moods. Starting out the day from this kind of stressed-out mindset only led me to feel more frustration, overwhelm, and anxiety as the day progressed.

Eventually, as the kids got older, I learned how to take a few moments to intentionally slow down each morning. I'd take long, deliberate deep breaths in and out, as the cortisol rose. I'd spend the morning hours slowing down on purpose, instead of getting caught up in the stress-induced frenzy.

Perhaps you can relate to this if you've ever "jumped out of bed in a panic" because of work, kids, travel, classes, meetings, events, or any other responsibility that caused you to feel that uncomfortable **cortisol awakening response**. Instead, the next time you start to feel the morning stress shoot way up, spend a few minutes consciously slowing yourself down with gentle thoughts. Take a few minutes to calmly plan out what the next step is. Remember to take things one step at a time, especially when it comes to mornings.

By practicing your **Morning Bookend steps** consistently, you'll be able to catch the cortisol before it drags down your entire day.

The Night Bookend

Now that you've completed everything you need to do for the day, it's time for the **Night Bookend** where you begin to wind down for the evening.

Step 1: The Stuff Round-Up

To begin the **Night Bookend**, start with **The Stuff Round-Up**. This is where you do a final sweep of your house, collecting random objects that are out of place and putting them back in their **Stuff Stations**. It's a way to mentally clear the decks before you turn down for the night.

Step 2: The Phone Time-Out

Instead of accidentally stimulating your brain with social media scrolling or by reading doom-inducing headlines, practice doing a nightly **phone time-out**. Try plugging in your phone on a charger in a different room where it's out of your line of view for 30 minutes or longer. Any time shorter than 30 minutes may not be enough time to fully disconnect from phone-related stress.

Neuroscience nugget: According to a study done at the University of London by Kepkee Loh, people who are always "juggling lots of different websites, apps, programs or other digital stimuli—tend to have less grey matter in a part of their brain involved with thought and emotion control. These same structural changes are associated with obsessive-compulsive disorder, depression, and anxiety disorders" (quoted in Heid, 2015).

If you already have an anxiety disorder, a lot of stress, or ADHD, scrolling through your phone all night long just might be exacerbating your symptoms. How about giving yourself a nightly **digital detox** to fully reset instead?

Step 3: "Do Nothing" Time

As someone who has experienced anxiety over the years, the one thing that really helped me learn to relax at night was establishing this firm rule with myself:

You have to allow yourself to "do nothing" at night.

Because I had been **chronically busy** for most of my life, I had never learned to allow myself to do nothing at night. Instead, I had accidentally trained my brain to use night-time to process and sort all the information from the day, to plan out tasks for the next week, and basically, to *think* myself awake for hours and hours.

After not sleeping well for many years, I eventually came to the conclusion that instead of telling my brain to do nothing at night, I was accidentally telling it that it should keep working non-stop.

Sometimes, we get into this habit because we think we can solve important problems while we're lying down in a quiet room with no other external distractions. It's like thinking of your brain as a problem detective on night-watch. However, at some point, I realized my nightly detective brain wasn't actually solving any real problems; all I was doing was wearing myself out. And so, I decided to quit my nightly problem-solving detective gig, and I made the consistent decision to wait until regular daytime hours to figure out solutions to problems instead.

When you feel the urge to solve problems at night, it can be helpful to tell yourself these gentle micro-thoughts:

"Night-time is for resting. I don't have to solve any problems right now."

"I've done enough for one day and it's okay to let myself rest."

"I don't need to do any more right now. The most important thing is to let my body reset itself."

If you want to lean into "doing nothing" at night more, it can be very helpful to practice **meditation**. An easy way to start is to listen to short guided meditations (you can find many free ones on YouTube). Guided meditations typically lead you through a restful story, or provide serene imagery for you to focus on, which tends to quiet the "mind chatter" down a bit. In this way, by focusing our ears, we can still our minds.

By staying in the moment with calming sounds, like a guided meditation, or focusing on white noise playing in the room, you are connecting with the present moment, instead of letting your brain jump around from past to future worries. It's creating a sense of stillness inside, building a sense of inner peace, and telling yourself it's okay to be calm for a little while.

By getting your brain to actively focus on tranquil sounds, you are practicing a form of mini-meditation.

Step 4: The Appreciation Journal

In my last book, *The Ultimate Anxiety Toolkit*, I wrote about keeping a daily **Appreciation Journal**. This is where you write 5–10 things you appreciate or feel grateful for as a nightly ritual. They can be tiny things or big things—as long as you connect with the feeling of appreciation when you write them down. This can be a calming way to close out the evening.

Write about the delicious sandwich you ate, the music you love, your cute pets, the technology you enjoy using every day, a nice walk you took, or any little thing that made you feel a surge of appreciation. When we practice gratitude, we actively raise our oxytocin levels, which is a neuro-peptide that causes our brains to feel love (Klein, 2014). Focusing on things you appreciate is a quick way to give your brain little love boosts each day.

By focusing on what's working out for us right now,
we are giving ourselves a positive mental boost.

Now that you've read these sample **Day Bookends,** try to custom-tailor ones that will work for you. Let's try easing in and out of our days in a calmer state of mind.

Worksheet: Write it out!

Using the ideas provided in this chapter, write out your **Morning** and **Night Bookend** steps. You can use the tools from the last few chapters as well as other self-care practices that work well for you.

For example:

Morning Bookend: The Negativity Neutralizer, Weekly Post-It, The Task Intensity Meter, stretching.

Night Bookend: Stuff Round-Up, **phone time-out**, **Appreciation Journal**, meditation.

After you've written down your steps, practice your **Day Bookends** for **two weeks consistently** and record the outcome below:

Morning Bookend:

1. . . . .

2. . . . .

3. . . . .

4. . . . .

Night Bookend:

1. . . . .

2. . . . .

3. . . . .

4. . . . .

Outcome:

. . . .

. . . .

— CHAPTER ROUND-UP —

☑ Simplify your to-do list using a **Weekly Post-It**.

☑ Keep **Time Containers** consistent each week.

☑ Use **color coding** to form brain associations.

☑ Develop a **long-term** approach to your stuff.

☑ Do an easy **Stuff Round-Up** each night.

☑ Use **Morning** and **Night Bookends** to start and end your day.

CHAPTER 3

When You Want to Feel Motivated...

* The Music Motivator
* The Wall Crusher
* The Intention Compass

THE MUSIC MOTIVATOR

Most people already accept that listening to relaxing music is a helpful way to de-stress and unwind. Maybe after a long work day you instinctively put on calming music for your drive home? Or perhaps you already have a workout playlist that helps you tackle the Stairmaster at the gym?

But did you know that music has the potential to motivate you to do specific tasks as well? If you learn to use **The Music Motivator** on a daily basis, you can train your brain to focus just by playing a particular song.

Neuroscience nugget: Researchers discovered that listening to fast-paced music increased participants' motivation to work out on exercise bikes, and that the faster the music, the faster people pedaled. In a different study in 2013, after listening to relaxing music, participants performed better overall on a stress test. And in a third study, researchers found that listening to upbeat music while also doing a task increased cognitive processing and provided memory benefits too (Cherry, 2019). Music can really affect our brains in motivating ways!

Classical conditioning was discovered by Ivan Pavlov, a Russian physiologist, who performed experiments on dogs' behavior. Using a buzzer sound to tell the dogs it was time to eat, the dogs quickly learned that hearing the buzzer noise meant that food would be served soon. Pavlov proved this was true by showing that when the buzzer sounded and there was no food delivered, the dogs would still salivate as though they were going to receive the food. Pavlov called this a **conditioned response**. He had created this brain association for the dogs:

So, knowing how easily we can condition brains using sound, how can we create a **conditioned response** in our brains using music to make us feel more motivated to do a task?

You've probably heard stories about how professional performers or athletes create pre-event rituals to "get ready to perform." For example, before competitions, track and field star Mohammed Ahmed listens to the same pre-game playlist that he has been using since high school, which includes the songs, "Lose Yourself" by Eminem and Mariah Carey's "Hero." He says these songs "internally instill self-belief" on race days (quoted in Bess and Briggins, 2016).

In this way, by using specific songs as a pre-performance mental association, Ahmed found a quick way to motivate his brain to complete **high-intensity tasks**, like competing in the Olympics.

What songs might already have a **mental motivation association** for you?

Use Music to Get Things Done

Since most of the time we're not competing in the Olympics, let's think about using **The Music Motivator** on a smaller scale to motivate us to do everyday tasks.

Think about a task that you are having trouble doing. To use this tool, you have to match a song with a task that energizes and motivates your brain to complete it.

Here are a few **Music Motivator** guidelines:

* For a task you are avoiding, pick an upbeat, energetic song that you enjoy.
* The song should have no other brain associations linked to it, especially negative ones. Also, lyrics can often be very distracting to our brains. Our prefrontal cortex has to work extra hard to drown out the distraction of catchy lyrics, and this can make our brains feel extra tired as a result (Shellenbarger, 2012).
* Choose a specific song that you are committing to using for this task as a consistent habit.

Here's an example from one client, who wanted to feel more motivated:

"I want to feel more motivated to clean the house because I often avoid doing it."

Then, she picked an upbeat genre of a music that she really enjoyed to play while doing the task:

"When I clean the house, I will now play Brazilian samba music."

We have now formed this association:

Samba = Cleaning

The upbeat music association worked well for her, and she no longer avoided cleaning on a regular basis when she played her cleaning playlist.

To use **The Music Motivator:**

* Put on the song, playlist, or album you picked to get your brain "in the mood" to do the task a few minutes before you start (in this client's case, it would be Samba music).
* Continue to listen to the music until you finish the task.
* When you're done, turn off the music.
* Now that you've cemented the music association in your brain, the more you remember to do it, the more it will stick!

If the particular song you picked is not working as a motivator, pick a different one! Keep trying until you find the *right match* to cue up your brain. Once you have found your song, however, keep using that exact same song, album, or playlist every time you want to do that particular task.

Here's another example from a client:

"I want to feel motivated to finish my midterm paper."

Music Motivator cue:

"I will listen to techno while I am writing my midterm paper."

Brain association formed:

Techno = Writing papers

One way to remember this is:

Choose specific songs to go with specific activities and repeat the songs every time you do the activity.

In this way, you're forming a clear connection for your brain to associate music with something you need to do.

Tracking Time with Songs

Sometimes, when I'm working on a task in a state of **fully focused attention,** my sense of passing time can get really wonky. For instance, when I'm deep into a writing project, I may think I've been writing for an hour, when in actuality, I've really been writing for two or three hours straight! Often this means I've ignored signs of exhaustion that I've been feeling in my body for hours and I've neglected taking any **Time Buffer breaks.**

> **Neuroscience nugget:** According to Dr. Ari Tuckman, this wonky time estimating is from something called "**time blindness,**" which can affect people with ADHD on a regular basis: "A good sense of time is one critical executive function. It involves knowing what time it is now, how much time is left, and how quickly time is passing. People with ADHD tend to be 'time blind,' meaning they aren't aware of the ticking of time" (Tuckman, 2021).

One way to combat **time blindness** is by using **The Music Motivator** to consistently track your time while doing tasks. If you're using the same playlist for the same task frequently, your brain will naturally start to grasp how much time is passing by noticing the length of the music.

I started using **The Music Motivator** as a way to get myself to write more consistently each week. I'd play Bach's *"Brandenburg Concertos"* album on my headphones, typing along to the music. Because the length of the album is about an hour long, my brain has now been programmed to write in hour-long segments, which feels like the ideal length of time for me to maintain my focus without feeling too tired or overwhelmed. When I hear the end of the album, I automatically remember to get up and take a break, too.

Neuroscience nugget: Did you know that classical music helps to stimulate the visual, auditory, and motor areas of the brain, which can be weaker in ADHD brains? According to a study done at the Eastman School of Music, students who "listened to classical music for 20 minutes a day had improved speech and language skills, a stronger memory, and greater organization of the brain" (Habermeyer, 2021).

What amount of time might work well for your brain in terms of task completion? Once you have an estimate, try to find a playlist or album that's approximately that length of time. Keep adjusting it until you find the match that works the best for you.

Some people use timers or alarms on their phone as a way to remind them of how much external time is passing. While this works for some people, others find phone alarms to be too intrusive to hear going off on a regular basis.

If this is the case for you, try programming your brain to do a task for the length of a particular playlist or album to guide you out of a fully focused state in an easier way.

Relax Your Brain Playlist

We can use music as a way to motivate ourselves to do tasks, and we can use music as a way to relax and reset our brains after work as well. One way to do this is to create a **Relax Your Brain** playlist. It can be helpful to keep this playlist separate from other ones that you use for different things.

Here are some rules for making a **Relax Your Brain** playlist:

* Pick calming, soothing music only.
* Typically, what works for people is music without lyrics, or music in a different language so that they won't get too fixated on the words or memory associations with the songs.
* Make sure the relaxing music playlist is different from your other playlists. Custom-tailor it to get your mind in a relaxing mood, not an energized one.
* Repeat the playlist every day for a week at the same time of day after work. See if it helps you remember to relax at the end of the day.

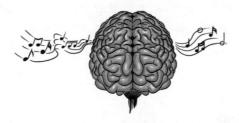

Now put on some music, and use it as a way to get your brain trained with sound!

Worksheet: Write it out!

Using the idea of a **conditioned response**, plan out what particular song you want to associate with doing a particular task. Try to create the brain association to "get ready" to do the task by playing the song each time you have to do the activity.

Example:

Describe the task and chosen song: "Whenever I clean the kitchen, I will put on Mozart."

Brain association: Mozart = Cleaning tasks.

Describe the task and the chosen song:

"Whenever I have to . . . . (task), I will listen to

. . . . (song)."

Brain association:

. . . . (song) = ... (task)

Describe the task and the chosen song:

"Whenever I have to . . . . (task), I will listen to

. . . . (song)."

Brain association:

. . . . (song) = ... (task)

Describe the task and the chosen song:

"Whenever I have to . . . . (task), I will listen to

. . . . (song)."

Brain association:

. . . . (song) = ... (task)

THE WALL CRUSHER

Sometimes, as we start to move towards starting a new goal, we accidentally trigger our own mental **wall of resistance**, which makes us feel stuck at the starting line. Imagine a brick wall springing up out of nowhere and blocking the goal path ahead:

What caused this wall to appear? Maybe you told your brain things about how "horrible" or "awful" the goal path ahead is, or perhaps you've told yourself, "I can't figure this out!" or "I'm going to screw it all up!" one too many times, and now...there's this looming wall in your way.

And it's not going to move...until you start to change your thoughts.

For many with anxiety, high stress levels, or ADHD, this **wall of resistance** can feel even more intimidating. Perhaps, growing up, you heard a lot of criticism about how you managed things, or you beat yourself up a lot for doing things in a way that you thought was "different" from others. Over the years, this may have caused you to tell yourself things like, "I can't manage this!" or "I'll never get it all done!" or "I'm bad at finishing tasks I start!"

On top of that, maybe you actively heard from other people, "You're not trying hard enough!" or "If you just focus harder, you'll get it done faster!"

While it's possible these people may have been trying to help you in their own (perhaps misguided) way, hearing a lot of this kind of criticism over time can make us repeat it to ourselves internally. We think thousands of thoughts each day (Murdock, 2020). If the majority of our daily thoughts are ones where we're beating ourselves up and criticizing ourselves, it's no wonder we sometimes feel stuck when we're facing a new challenge.

Because you've told yourself so many times that you can't figure things out (despite the fact that you actually have already figured out many things before), you may now believe this to be true. That's precisely why the **wall of resistance** is now standing there. And it won't budge until you start to shift your self-talk a little.

The good news is we can change our self-talk, one thought at a time. You can think of it like this:

Every small thought you change in a positive direction can have a big overall impact on your emotional state.

So how do we start to tear down our own **wall of resistance?**

We break it down one brick at a time, using the strength of **motivational self-talk,** which is an amazing power tool to have on hand. Positive self-talk is the most effective **Wall Crusher** out there. And it's completely generated by you. You are the one supplying the power. Turn it on full blast, and watch that wall turn to dust! Do it a little at a time, and the wall comes apart, brick by brick.

Neuroscience nugget: Psychology researchers at Carnegie Mellon University in Pittsburgh found that stressed-out participants who were told to give themselves self-praise affirmations during a problem-solving test did better overall than those who didn't. The researchers concluded that, "self-affirmations can buffer the effects of chronic stress on actual problem-solving" (Creswell *et al.*, 2013).

The way we talk to ourselves is important. If we have a lot of negative self-talk going on, we can start to change it, one tiny **micro-thought** at a time.

Trip-Wiring the Wall

Sometimes, even hearing the phrase "positive self-talk" is enough to trip-wire people's **wall of resistance**. The word "positive" can make some think that they have to think thoughts that sound unattainable to them such as, "I'm amazing!" or "I'm doing so great!"

While these thoughts can be helpful to get to eventually, you might want to take things a little slower to begin with. Start by gently telling yourself kinder **micro-thoughts** more consistently each day. The more frequently you can repeat them, the quicker you're breaking your old negative self-talk habit.

You are supplying the motivational power with repetition and consistency.

Here are some gentle **self-talk micro-thoughts** that might help you take that wall down, brick by brick. Try them out and see which ones "click" for you:

> *"I'm figuring it out, one step at a time."*
>
> *"I only have to take the first small step forward and then I will figure out the rest as I go."*
>
> *"I'm handling things one task at a time."*
>
> *"I've figured out new things before and I'll figure out new things again."*
>
> *"Each week, I'm getting better at figuring out new challenges as they appear."*
>
> *"I am picturing how great I'm going to feel when I figure this all out."*
>
> *"Taking small steps each week will add up over time."*

And then, add a closing thought such as:

> *"It's okay to go at my own pace."*

You really can go at your own pace. You are not in a race with anyone but yourself.

Why even make it a race at all? Go at your own pace; move forward a little at a time. You can control what steps you are taking forward each week. As long as you're taking consistent steps forward, trust that you will get to where you want to go.

Turn Your Mindset Around

Motivational self-talk can help us feel more empowered to break down our own mental resistance. However, when we start beating ourselves up with negative self-talk and criticism again, the wall in front of us starts to quickly rebuild itself, resetting that resistance.

When you feel this happening, practice a few of your gentler self-talk thoughts to knock the **wall of resistance** back down again. The more you practice catching the self-criticism at the onset, the quicker you can turn your mindset around and get yourself back on track.

It's a mental choice you can make in the moment to be kinder to yourself. Trust that there are positive benefits of doing this, and that it will eventually lead you to a much better emotional place, even if it feels really uncomfortable at first.

It can be helpful to remember:

All new habits feel uncomfortable at first until they don't feel new anymore.

Once the habit doesn't feel new, you will no longer feel uncomfortable doing it.

So, instead of saying: "I'm not getting there fast enough!"

Say: "I'm figuring things out one thing at a time. I'm going at my own pace."

Instead of saying: "I don't know how to do this!"

Say: "I've figured out things before. This is just a new thing I'm learning how to do. I'll figure it out soon enough."

Tell yourself you're figuring it out one small step at a time, one day at a time, one week at a time.

You are the one supplying the power to make this tool work. Go on and crank it up with some consistency!

Worksheet: Write it out!

Practice taking down your **wall of resistance** using frequent motivational self-talk phrases.

Write out three phrases that work for you to repeat consistently throughout the day:

1. I am learning how to...

. . . .

. . . .

. . . .

. . . .

2. I am figuring out...

. . . .

. . . .

. . . .

. . . .

3. I am getting good at...

. . . .

. . . .

. . . .

. . . .

Now write out a few of your own:

1. . . . .

. . . .

. . . .

. . . .

2. . . . .

. . . .

. . . .

. . . .

3. . . . .

. . . .

. . . .

. . . .

THE INTENTION COMPASS

Now that we've crushed our mental **wall of resistance**, we can now move on to a **goal-setting warm-up** to get you feeling more motivated. I call this tool **The Intention Compass**. Think of it as setting course before you start your journey. It's like programming your mental GPS for your intended destination before you step on the gas!

To use this tool, write out this question to ask yourself before taking on a new goal:

"Why do I want to accomplish this goal?"

And then, answer the question by writing out *one simple sentence* that clarifies what your intention is. Getting clear about why you want to do something really helps fire up the motivation engine, and it also makes it easier for our brain to make decisions going forward.

Often, our attention is **unfocused** towards a goal because we haven't clarified what exactly our intention is. We "sort of" know why we want to do something, but we haven't stated it to ourselves in a simple sentence that our brain clearly understands. It's helpful to remember:

Your brain is always listening to what you tell it to do.

Should I start or stop? Should I go down this path or stay still? Do I want this thing or don't I?

Sometimes, you've issued too many commands to your brain's computer that cancel each other out and now you're stuck, staring at a spinning wheel on the screen as it tries to process all the conflicting information. You may "sort of" want to accomplish your goal, but you also "sort of" don't want to get started. We've all been there!

You can often find the motivation you need by simply telling yourself *why* you want to move forward.

Tell yourself why you want to accomplish your goal in one simple sentence to boost your motivation.

Helping Others

Many people find that if they can state an intention that involves helping people or providing a clear service that's needed in some way, it makes the motivation kick in faster. When we think about how we can *help* people by doing something, this can give us a real **sense of purpose**, which is often the fastest way to motivate ourselves.

Neuroscience nugget: Did you know that helping others can also help our brains? Researchers Jamil Zaki and Jason P. Mitchell asked participants to make decisions with money that they could give out to other participants or keep for themselves, with no other instructions. When participants shared the money with other participants, there was increased activity in the orbitofrontal cortex (OFC) area of the brain, which created a feeling of reward and pleasure. The researchers found that, "Remarkably, the lowest OFC response was observed when participants chose to allocate money inequitably to themselves" (Zaki and Mitchell, 2011, p.19762).

In other words, finding ways that our goals can benefit both ourselves *and* others can give us the motivational brain boost to start moving forward.

When we're thinking of an end goal as being something that will impress people instead of benefit them, it's altogether too easy to become overly concerned with what other people think and to start criticizing ourselves before we even begin.

In this way, our **inner critic** can quickly stomp on the brakes, halting any steps toward our goal.

You can remember it like this:

Unleashing your harsh inner critic is the quickest way to stop moving toward a goal.

When we make our goals about getting approval from other people, it typically fires up our **inner fears** rather than firing up our **inner strengths** to complete something.

Personal Growth and Future Feelings

You can also make your intention about helping yourself grow in some way. For instance, maybe you want to finish a painting because you would like to put the idea that's been nagging you for years to rest. You might say to yourself: "My intention for painting this is to get this idea out of my head and onto the canvas so that I can focus on new ideas."

Sometimes, the idea of finally "getting the idea out into the world" so that you can "do other things" can be a very motivating intention for finishing projects—because, in this way, you are helping *yourself* to process something and move on.

If you want to add another sentence about what will happen as a result of you getting it out on the canvas, you could earn yourself some extra motivation points: "When I finish this painting, it will make people feel interested in the subject matter I am showing them. This would make me feel good to provide this to them." Now it feels even more motivating to start moving.

When I have worked with university students who feel "stuck with senioritis" because their last semester suddenly feels really difficult to complete, it's helpful to find a clear intention to get through it. Sometimes, filling out this sentence with an intention can really help get you focused on the finish line: "My intention for graduating school is so that I can get this degree in _____ and then help people afterward by _____." This helps us focus our attention on why we need to complete the goal, and also helps us connect with what's coming afterward—especially when we've temporarily lost sight of the destination.

Add on how you would like to feel (in a positive way) and you will give yourself a powerful motivation boost. For example: "My intention is to do _____ so I can help people _____ and this will make me feel _____."

You can think of it like this:

Use picturing the future feeling you want to feel as your personal motivation tool.

Intentions for Everyday Goals

While intention setting can work well for big milestone goals, it can also help motivate you to do smaller everyday tasks as well.

Even something as mundane and ordinary as doing a mountain of laundry for your household might make you feel stuck. For this task, there's no need to journal; you could simply state out your intention in your head before you start: "My intention for getting through this pile of laundry today is to provide my family with clean clothes for the week." And then, if that doesn't motivate you, you can add a thought about how it will make your family feel: "My family will feel better having clean nice clothes to wear this week which will make me feel good too." Now you've set your **Intention Compass,** and you know what to do.

Something about clearly stating your own intention can signal to your brain that you've now made a clear decision about moving forward with it.

In other words, you've just given yourself the mental **green light** to go!

Worksheet: Write it out!

Before you take on a new goal, clearly write out your intention in one simple sentence using the template provided below. When you clearly state your intention, you're giving yourself a mental green light to move ahead.

Write out your intention below:

My intention in completing . . . . is to help people

. . . . and to feel . . . .

Now try writing out intentions for a few goals you would like to set for yourself:

1. . . . .

. . . .

. . . .

. . . .

2. . . . .

. . . .

. . . .

. . . .

3. . . . .

. . . .

. . . .

. . . .

— CHAPTER ROUND-UP —

☑ Condition your brain to do tasks with music.

☑ Use **motivational self-talk** frequently.

☑ The words you tell yourself are important.

☑ Write down your **intention** for accomplishing a goal.

☑ Use **future feelings** and **helping others** as motivators.

CHAPTER 4

When You Want to Achieve Your Goals...

* The Goal Splicer
* The Goal Sponsor
* The Goal Tracker
* The Reward Planner

THE GOAL SPLICER

When I was a little kid, I really enjoyed the idea of getting rewards (like glitter star stickers) for accomplishing goals in school. I liked stickers back then, it was pretty much all the motivation I needed. Clean your desk! Do I get a puffy sticker? Finish this math test! Well, since you're giving me a *unicorn* sticker...

As I got older, there were fewer outside rewards given (and I no longer craved unicorn stickers), and as I hadn't learned to generate my own mental rewards for anything I did, my goal setting took on a more anxious turn. I often stressed myself out with goals that were too big to tackle or wore myself out from trying to do too much over short periods of time. All of this frequently resulted in me feeling completely burnt out and unmotivated.

Maybe you can relate to this in some way?

Years later, as I was developing tools to help people who were having similar problems, I found a way to approach goals that felt way less overwhelming and stress inducing:

Set smaller weekly goals and take them one step at a time.

By breaking things down into small steps that feel more manageable to tackle each week, we can feel less stressed out and more motivated about completing our goals.

How Do You Feel About Your Goal?

When we convince our brains that a task will be "fun" to complete or "good" for us to do in a motivating way, we increase our chances of actually completing the goal.

Neuroscience nugget: Studies have shown that the amygdala (which triggers emotions) and the frontal lobe (which processes information and forms strategies) communicate with each other in different ways depending on how we actually *feel* about the goal. In a recent study, researchers found that if people felt very motivated to achieve their goal, this led them to view the goal as easier to accomplish and less difficult to do (Cole, Balcetis, and Zhang, 2013).

An easy way to remember this is:

Positive emotions about goal = Improves chances of completion

Your emotions can either move you quickly toward your goal, or stop progress altogether, depending on what you are choosing to *feel*.

When Goal Setting Goes Wrong

When we feel negative emotions about taking the first step towards a goal, it's typically because we've told ourselves that we have to accomplish *too big* a goal in *too short* an amount of time. Frequently, when asked what goals they would like to work on, clients will tell me their huge, monumental, stressful-sounding goals that they also want to accomplish instantly (which makes them anxious to even think about). As a result of these overly daunting expectations, many people often get stuck at the starting line and never start moving toward their goals.

To solve this problem, I came up with a tool called **The Goal Splicer**.

This tool takes a huge-sounding goal, such as "I will write an entire screenplay in two months!" and splices it down to a more reasonable, smaller goal that someone will actually do (for example: "I will write one scene a week").

This is how we create a **micro-goal** that feels more fun and manageable to do, so that we actually *want* to start doing it.

Here's how **goal splicing** works:

1. Take your goal.
2. Cut it down by half (or whatever percentage feels right to you).
3. Say your new goal to yourself and see if it now feels more manageable to do.
4. If it doesn't, do a final splice down until it works for you.
5. Stop when you've arrived at a **micro-goal** that feels easy to start.

You don't want to splice the goal down to nothing as that won't get you moving, but you also don't want to splice it down to something that *still* feels scary and resistance triggering! You want to find the happy middle ground in between.

Here's an example of how to go about splicing your goal down until it feels manageable:

Client: "I need to start running ten miles every day of the week."

Me as goal splicer: "How about we take that goal and cut it down a bit? Maybe by half to start?"

Client: "Sure...maybe...five miles? I'm not sure..." [Typically, indecision means more goal splicing is required.]

Goal splicer: "How about we cut it down further? How about one mile?"

Client: "One mile is way too little for me. It's not challenging enough at all. Two miles feels better to me. How about two miles twice a week?" [This is positive progress because it sounds like they're starting to goal splice on their own.]

Goal splicer: "Does two miles twice a week sound reasonable to you?"

Client: "Yes, no problem. I can start on Monday and then do Wednesday after that."

Goal splicer: "Are you sure that doesn't sound like too much?" [Sometimes, at this point, clients will continue to **goal splice** down until we get there.]

Client: "Yes, that sounds great. I'm going to start this Monday." [You will know you have arrived at your final destination because you've set a date to start.]

On my side of things, I am just trying to tease out the answer they already know in their gut by asking questions in a non-biased way. We already know how much we can do each day, we already know what feels easy to us to do, and we already know what's a good starting place that isn't too overwhelming. Sometimes, it just takes a little prompting to get yourself to realize what you already internally know.

Here's another example from a client:

Client: "My goal is to clear out the spare bedroom and turn it into an office by the end of this week."

Me as goal splicer: "How about we break that goal down first, and then figure out a reasonable time frame after we know the weekly steps?" [Sometimes, it's good to splice your goal down first and then figure out how long it will actually take to accomplish. When it comes to reorganizing a room in your home, it can often be easy to underestimate how long this will take to do.]

Client: "My spare room actually has a lot of old stuff and storage boxes packed into it. Just clearing that stuff out and selling it online or donating it will probably take a few weeks."

Goal splicer: "How many things can you clear out per week realistically?"

Client: "Realistically, with work and everything else on my plate, I think I can only manage a few boxes each weekend."

Goal splicer: "And how many boxes total do you think there are to clear out in the entire room?"

Client: "Probably about 10 boxes worth of stuff. Maybe more."

Goal splicer: "So, if you're taking out a few boxes each weekend, that sounds like it might be at least a month's worth of work, maybe more. How long will it take to organize the empty room into an office?"

Client: "At least a few weeks because I have to figure out where everything goes and move some new furniture in there."

Goal splicer: "Is it possible that giving yourself a few months to do this reorganization project might be a better time frame to work within rather than a week? How much time do you think you will need?"

Client: "I think giving myself two months to complete it sounds more reasonable. I can start with a few boxes this weekend." [In this case, we've arrived at our destination when the time frame to complete the task has become clearer based on the small steps we've established.]

Sometimes, we don't really give ourselves enough time to complete large tasks. After you've goal-spliced your goal down into manageable weekly steps, you'll be able to get a better **time perspective** on how long you actually need to complete the entire task.

For my clients, I act as their initial **goal splicer** (and then later as their **goal sponsor**), but there's no reason you can't be your own **goal splicer** by asking yourself enough questions until you get there.

Here are some questions to ask yourself:

* "How can I cut this goal down to a more manageable size?"
* "Is the new amount *reasonable* to expect myself to do (given my other time commitments and schedule) consistently over a period of time?"
* "Do I feel better and more motivated about starting the new micro-goal?" (If not, repeat the steps until you get the goal down far enough.) You will know when it feels right to you.

Splicing goal = Splices mental resistance

The result of effective goal splicing is: A reasonable-sounding micro-goal that starts to turn the mental wall of resistance to rubble!

Worksheet: Write it out!

To use this tool, select a small goal you would like to work on.

Write your goal here:

....

....

....

....

....

....

Splice your goal down a little. Try cutting it down until it feels manageable to start doing:

....

....

....

....

....

....

....

Write out your new micro-goal and write out the day/time you will do it:

....

....

☆

THE GOAL SPONSOR

To keep our confidence flying high in relation to accomplishing our goal, and to keep that brick **wall of resistance** crumbling, we're going to need to use the next tool called **The Goal Sponsor**. This gives us a surge of motivation supplied by **consistency** and **accountability** for our goal journey ahead.

The first time I was paid to write a magazine article, I froze up at the starting line. Like a deer in headlights, I found myself staring at the blank page on my screen, wondering how I was going to write a sentence, and how I had ever written a sentence before.

Although I had clearly written some sentences at some point in life, this was a new "paid" assignment, which was somehow enough to weird me out, mostly because of it being a new thing. And, as I often tell people:

New experiences = Anxiety

This is true for all new experiences, even good ones. There's always some level of anxiety experienced because it's a new thing that you haven't figured out yet. Even if you were to win the lottery, after the initial surge of adrenaline and excitement, you might possibly feel a wave of panic wash over you, followed by anxiety over what to do next.

It's all down to the **newness factor**. Once it no longer feels new, chances are, you won't feel as anxious about it anymore. Sometimes, what you need to overcome this newness factor is a little **accountability**.

After a few weeks of being completely stuck at the starting line of my article, I called up my good friend, educational therapist and fellow author,

Ezra Werb, and I told him I had not even written a single sentence yet. All he said back was, "Send me the first page when you're done and I'll read it!"

And somehow, like magic, that worked. I got off the phone and instantly thought, "Well, I better send him some pages..." And then, I was off typing, just like that.

Why did this work? I had found accountability, which gave me the energy boost to take the first step forward. Accountability means you've found a witness to watch you reach your goal. It's the missing piece you might be searching for if **goal splicing** isn't enough to get you moving forward.

Goal splicing + Accountability = Crushes mental resistance

When I work with clients, we start off with small weekly goals and I provide consistent accountability as they reach their **goal markers** each week. What I find is that it isn't too long before the momentum builds and clients start speeding toward the finish line of their goals.

> **Neuroscience nugget:** In a study on accountability done at the American Society of Training and Development, 65% of participants completed their goal if they committed to doing it by telling a partner. When participants had a regular accountability appointment with this partner, 95% of participants completed their goal (Oppong, 2017).

In other words, it can be *really* helpful to tell someone your goal progress each week.

You might remember it like this:

By announcing our goal progress to someone,
we're bringing it from the
world of the intangible
to the tangible.

Now that another human is clearly involved as a witness, we can't just hide away in our own heads with our own ideas, bumping into our own **wall of resistance** over and over again. Just knowing that there is now someone else involved in the process is usually enough for us to find the courage to take the first step.

Accountability pushes us to step outside of our comfort zone,
giving us the needed motivational boost to take action.

How to Find a Goal Sponsor

Over the years, I've learned that it matters who you pick to be your **goal sponsor** for your particular goal, if you want the process to actually work. So how can we find the most beneficial **goal sponsor** for our needs?

* Pick a person with a positive mindset. Pick someone who is (at least, the majority of time) positive, upbeat, and encouraging to be your **goal sponsor**. Often, people want to pick their relatives. This is fine, if your relatives meet these criteria. However, if you've never received your dad's approval in the past, why would you pick him now to sponsor your new goal? Ask yourself: "Is this a way of accidentally triggering my **wall of resistance** and blocking my own path?"

* Try to pick someone who has done something already on the path you're on. Ideally, it's good to ask find someone who is further along the goal path that you want to go down. This way, they will have the wisdom of the goal journey ahead and some understanding of what the process feels like to emotionally navigate.

* Make it a fair exchange of positivity. If you are requiring non-stop goal sponsoring while giving nothing back in return, it's an uneven equation. While you might find a few kind people who can weather this scenario once or twice, they certainly won't weather it endlessly. Ideally, a goal sponsoring system works best when both people can sponsor each other's goals in the same way. If that's not possible, expressing your genuine gratitude and appreciation can be beneficial for all parties involved.

When You're Stuck Finding a Sponsor

If you can't find someone around who is the right fit for your goal, try hiring a coach or a therapist who specializes in goal setting to work with you on getting started. There are also many online workshops you can sign up for where people work on goals together.

It takes a little bravery to admit to strangers that you're stuck, but it can also help to normalize your feelings when you hear that others are experiencing similar things. It's helpful to remind yourself:

Every small step you take forward leads you to a different outcome.

By telling someone your goal and reporting your progress consistently, you are tipping the chances of goal completion in your favor. If you're stuck finding a goal group, then, try using the next tool, **The Goal Tracker**, as an easy way to start providing accountability to yourself each week.

Worksheet: Write it out!

Pick a specific goal you want to work on and use **The Goal Splicer** and **The Goal Sponsor** tools to plan it out:

. . . .

. . . .

Goal I want to work on (be specific—splice it down to make it feel doable):

. . . .

. . . .

Start date for this goal:

. . . .

. . . .

My goal sponsor for this goal:

. . . .

. . . .

What are three *small* steps I can take to start moving toward this goal?

1. . . . .

2. . . . .

3. . . . .

What will I do to hold myself accountable for completing these three steps?

. . . .

. . . .

THE GOAL TRACKER

I've noticed that there are two common problems that happen after people finally accomplish their goals: They quickly forget most of the small steps they took to accomplish their goal, and then, they quickly forget to emotionally celebrate what they just did.

Basically, in getting to the end of your goal, you forget most of what it took to get there and then you also don't really let yourself enjoy the result.

Why is this a problem? For these reasons:

* In forgetting how you got there, you aren't fully acknowledging all of the many little steps it took to get to your goal. So, the next time you're starting out from scratch, it's easy to feel overwhelmed all over again.
* If you don't emotionally celebrate your accomplishments after they happen, you are not giving yourself a chance to ever really connect with the *feeling* of accomplishment.
* Instead of getting a dopamine boost from accomplishing your goal, you've now created no clear reward for finishing the task at all. This can lead to feelings of low self-esteem rather than getting that super-charged self-esteem boost from goal completion.

We tend to forget many things unless we're actively tracking them somewhere. If I were to ask you to remember what you did last year, chances are you would list about 4–5 things. And you certainly did *way* more than 4–5 things over the course of one year.

When we track things and write them down, we can emotionally connect more with what we have done. It's like marking that positive memory with a highlighter pen:

> **Neuroscience nugget:** According to writer Mark Murphy, writing things down helps our brains to remember them more: "Encoding is the biological process by which the things we perceive travel to our brain's hippocampus where they're analyzed. From there, decisions are made about what gets stored in our long-term memory and, in turn, what gets discarded. Writing improves that encoding process" (Murphy, 2018).

After we accomplish a goal, how can we find a way to better preserve the memory of that particular accomplishment in our brains?

Tracking Your Progress

Because I witnessed this type of "accomplishment erasure" problem happening to so many people, especially **Chronically Busy People,** I came up with **The Goal Tracker.**

The Goal Tracker uses a simple **bullet journaling system** to keep track of where you are each day with your goals, and to track your goal progress over a longer period of time.

To start with, find a blank journal. At the top of the page, put the date. Then, underneath, write out the small steps you took that day toward your goal in bullet list form. Bullet lists help us keep our journal short and sweet, which, over time, makes it easier to keep using the system consistently every day. Also, visually, it's easier to track a bullet list over a longer period of time than it is to have to scan through many months of lengthy paragraphs.

Let's get started with this simple system of tracking our goals by looking at two examples. Here is a **Goal Tracker** example from a client who was searching for a new job:

Monday:

* I fixed up my resume.
* I emailed my resume to my ex-colleague to double check it.
* I found three jobs to apply for.

And here is a **goal tracking** example from a client who started a new online business:

Monday:

* I reviewed similar websites.
* I looked at sample logo designs.
* I received a few quotes from website designers.

Every day, both of these clients tracked the small steps they took. They didn't always have three things on their list; sometimes they only did one thing, and that's okay! The most important part of this exercise is consistency. **Write something down each day.** That's how we practice connecting emotionally with every small step we take forward.

We have to practice feeling positive emotions in small doses in order to feel positive emotions in big doses later.

Over time, you'll start to see your progress, and you'll also be able to recall all the little steps you've taken to get there with more clarity.

The Bigger Picture

At the end of each month, take a few minutes to review your **goal-tracking journal**. Flip through the pages for that month and read all the steps that you completed to help you remember all the tiny steps you took to walk yourself across the goal's finish line. Appreciate how many goal markers you reached, and how consistently you were reaching them. The longer you keep your **goal-tracking journal,** the more you will begin to be able to see how far you've progressed over a longer period of time. You'll also start to get a sense of the **bigger picture of time,** and how things are actually happening for you, even on days when it didn't feel like they were.

This is how we build a better **long-term time perspective,** which helps us feel more motivated to keep going forward with our goals.

Reaching Goal Markers

As you keep your **goal-tracking journal,** be sure to clearly note when you reach a **goal marker**.

Goal markers are big steps toward your goal. And eventually, your **final goal marker** will be when you complete your goal and cross the finish line!

Imagine them to be like red flags that you dot along your journaling pathway to mark significant positive points in time.

You can notate your goal markers in a number of creative ways. The way I personally notate goal markers in my **goal-tracking journal** is to draw a line underneath my daily bullet list toward the bottom of the page, and then write the goal marker out in capital letters. This way I can clearly see the goal markers on the page—they jump out at me and make me notice them.

For example, if the client searching for a job managed to secure an interview, their goal marker would look like this:

Friday:

* Sent out a cover letter and resume to old supervisor.
* Updated LinkedIn resume.
* GOT INTERVIEW!

Or, the client who was starting a business might note their goal marker like this:

Friday:

* Uploaded new photos to website.
* Updated online shop information.
* RECEIVED FIRST ORDER FOR STORE!

Make it fun to note your progress in your **goal-tracking journal** by getting creative in a visual way. Some people who are more artistically inclined draw out pictures next to their list; others like to use different colors to notate different types of goals; some use stickers as a way to make it more fun (go ahead and use the glitter star stickers you loved as a kid if it makes you feel good). Keep it simple to start with, and then, see where the process takes you.

Once you see it all written down in front of you, you'll find that you *actually* do quite a lot each month. It's an easy way to remember to give yourself credit for all the small goal steps you're taking. Give it a try for a few weeks in a row and see how it works for you, in terms of motivation.

Remember: Keep it simple, keep it fun!

Worksheet: Write it out!

Using the **goal tracking journal**, write out three small steps you took today. If you accomplished a **goal marker**, highlight it at the bottom with a star! And then, remember to build in some motivational self-talk such as, "I feel so relieved that I've finished this goal" and "I'm proud of what I've just achieved" when you cross the goal's finish line!

Day of the week:

Goal I am working on:

* Step:

* Step:

* Step:

☑ GOAL MARKER

THE REWARD PLANNER

Have you ever raced from goal to goal without ever pausing to stop and think about what you just accomplished? After completing a goal, have you ever found yourself thinking something dismissive like, "Well, that's done. What's next?"

While setting and achieving small goals can potentially boost our self-esteem, burning ourselves out from goal-related stress can have a negative effect on our emotions. This can happen when we're not allowing ourselves enough **Time Buffers** in between goals to decompress, and when we're not giving ourselves any **mental rewards** for completing things.

We're in such a hurry all the time to complete so many tasks that we often miss the opportunity to feel the relief of finishing any of them, because we're off rushing to the next goal, much like a **Goal Robot:**

The **Goal Robot** has such an endless to-do list, that there's no time to pause and reflect upon any progress that has been made. The **Goal Robot** just wants to keep going and going...until it collapses from exhaustion and its batteries run out.

What's your **Goal Robot** mode like? Sometimes, I turn into "Mom Robot" when I'm racing around trying to get things sorted for my kids, making meals, cleaning, and trying to stay on top of my family's schedules. After I complete one thing, I often catch myself thinking "What's next?" instead of pausing, taking a deep breath, and feeling accomplished about anything I have just done.

You will know you're in "robot mode" when it feels like you're rushing through things on auto-pilot, you're not taking stock of how tired you are, and you're not emotionally connecting with finishing tasks at all.

It can be helpful to give your **Goal Robot** a name so that you can catch yourself more easily whenever you accidentally activate "robot mode" throughout your day. This allows you to become a mindful observer of what you're doing, which gives you an opportunity to pause and redirect your behavior in a more positive direction.

You can think, "Oh, there I go again, I'm acting like 'Work Robot' and forgetting to take a lunch break again!" or something like this, to gain some perspective on what you're doing while you're doing it.

We're often raised to believe that if we don't keep working hard non-stop, that nothing good will happen for us. And as a result of this faulty core belief, we tend to feel a sense of shame if we pause the **Goal Robot** cycle for even a brief moment. If this is a core belief you are holding, it can be helpful to ask yourself, "Do I want to keep believing this to be true? How might it be affecting my emotional state?"

It's helpful to remember:

You have to allow yourself to feel proud of yourself.

Start by practicing feeling proud of yourself, one small goal at a time.

Deactivating Robot Mode

Here is a simple tool to deactivate "robot mode" and connect with the feelings of relief, pride, and accomplishment: **The Reward Planner**. Using this tool, you will plan small rewards for every **goal marker** that you hit. You can remember this image:

* Each time you hit a **goal marker** in your **goal tracking journal**, give yourself a **reward** of some kind.
* For smaller goal markers, plan smaller rewards.
* For bigger goal markers, plan bigger rewards.
* Record what reward you gave yourself for each specific goal marker in your daily **goal tracking journal**.

Planning Rewards

For this exercise, rewards should be things you can do on your own that don't involve other people. Often, people want to pick rewards like "Dinner with my friends," and then they'll get stuck when their friends can't make it on that particular day, and as a result, they won't give themselves *any* reward at all.

Ideally, rewards should be about *you* celebrating your own successes for *you*, not for anyone else. This doesn't mean that for bigger goal markers you can't plan a celebration party with friends—however, it might be helpful to call this a bonus reward rather than a main reward.

For instance, a client recently finished his dissertation, which had taken him many years to complete. He planned a party with his friends to celebrate, which was going to happen a few days afterwards. I told him that sounded great, but that we should label this a **bonus reward**.

I asked him, "What do you want as a separate reward for finishing that you can do on your own today?"

He thought about it and said he wanted to visit a museum, eat at his favorite restaurant, and watch his favorite TV show. He listed those three things together to make it seem more unique and specific as a way to remember the achievement.

We used **The Reward Planner** to map these steps out clearly:

Goal completed: Finished my dissertation.

My reward: Today: Go to museum, eat Thai food, watch favorite TV show.

Bonus reward: Saturday: Have party at my house with friends.

This way, he had a clear idea of an **associated reward** he was going to do right away to celebrate. Then, on Saturday, he could enjoy a bonus reward to further mark the occasion.

You can think of it like this:

Give yourself the feelings you want to feel first before you involve other people in the process.

Practice celebrating your successes for *you*, and not for other people. Start believing you are worthy of your own support and praise...because you are!

Picture What You Want to Feel

Another client was completing a big time-consuming project for work.

She had been working long hours and lots of overtime, and was feeling completely mentally drained.

To get through the last week of the project, I had her plan out her **goal reward** ahead of time, so she could use it as a way to visualize the end of the project. It took us a while to figure out what would be a fun reward to do on her own, mostly because she was so exhausted it was hard to remember what was fun anymore.

"Nothing feels fun right now," she sighed, "I can't even picture what I want to do and I can't even picture the project being over!"

I asked her, where did she want to be sitting to enjoy completing the project? What would she be looking at that would make her feel relieved it was over?

After some consideration, she replied, "I see myself sitting by the ocean enjoying the sunset…"

"What will you feel emotionally when you sit on the beach at sunset?" I asked.

"Relief!" she said, "I will definitely feel relieved and happy that this project is over!"

So, we went with that image! I told her to hold onto the image in her head as though it was a photograph she was looking at. And every time she was stressed that week, she pictured that mental photo of herself sitting on the beach, feeling a sense of "relief" and "completion":

In this way, she was rehearsing how she wanted to feel after she was done. One way to remember this is:

Practice feeling the feelings you want to feel by visualizing yourself feeling that way in the near future.

By doing this, you are using your imagination to picture the emotions you want to feel: Happiness, relief, accomplishment. Hold that image in your mind. By holding it for a few seconds at a time in your mind, you are rehearsing those specific feelings. And by rehearsing those specific feelings, you are training your brain to feel them later in larger doses when you actually complete your goal. See your feelings as something you have to practice in tiny doses before you can feel them in big doses.

Using this approach to your feelings will change your perspective on many things and help you connect with what you want to feel more often, rather than waiting to do it later. Practice feeling happier smaller moments more frequently, rather than holding off on feeling happy until only big things happen for you.

Pick Something Unique and Specific

A helpful guideline for choosing a goal reward is to pick something **unique** and **specific** to do. When you hold the mental image in your mind it should be a very specific one (for example: Sitting by the ocean at sunset) and it should be unique, in that, you don't do it every day already. You don't have to plan overly extravagant, elaborate, or expensive rewards. It's more important to focus on connecting with the feeling of the reward, instead. Ask yourself: "How do I want to feel when I am experiencing the reward?"

And you don't have to spend a lot of money to feel happy, proud, or relieved that you finished your goal. You just have to *give yourself permission* to feel those feelings.

Sometimes, for simpler rewards, you can just **delay gratification** of something like watching your favorite TV show or buying yourself a new video game. This means that you would have to hold off on doing this specific thing until *after* you completed your **goal marker**. That way, it gives you something to look forward to, and to mentally hold onto, as a symbol of completion.

You will have formed this mental equation:

$$\text{Task completed} = \text{Specific reward}$$

For bigger goal markers, plan bigger rewards. For smaller goal markers, plan smaller rewards. And for all rewards, plan ones that feel manageable to do, so that you will actually do them.

Reward Follow-Through

Sometimes, clients will really enjoy planning out their reward for a goal marker in our sessions, but then, after they've completed the goal, they will completely forget to do the reward.

Imagine if you promised your pet dog a treat for rolling over, and then the dog rolled over, and you just walked away and forgot to give them the treat? Your pet dog would be really disappointed! And the next time you asked the dog to roll over, they might not want to do it again.

This is what your brain feels like when you don't pause and acknowledge that it just got you through a really hard task. As a result, it might feel less motivated the next time you ask it to do another really hard task. Lo and behold, you might find yourself staring at that mental **wall of resistance** the next time you try to get started on working toward a new goal.

You can avoid this dopamine roller coaster (and the **wall of resistance**) by actually following through on your reward.

It can be helpful to ask yourself a few questions as you plan your reward:

* "Will I actually do this reward after my goal is complete?"
* "Is this reward easy and fun for me to complete on my own?"
* "Do I want to make my reward more manageable so that I can follow through on it?"
* "Does this reward feel positive and healthy for my brain and body to do?"

Perhaps something like driving to the ocean is too ambitious when you're already exhausted from completing your goal. If this is the case, pick an easier reward for yourself to do. Pick something that sounds fun, doesn't require a huge amount of energy, and that is something you will actually complete.

Rewards are a simple way of thanking your brain. By thanking your brain more frequently, your brain will then thank you with a happier emotional state.

Worksheet: Draw it out!

Think about an upcoming goal or task that you want to complete. Now, imagine a **unique** and **specific** reward that you can give yourself that you will do after you complete the goal.

In the space below, draw out the reward as a specific image (for example: Watching the sunset at the beach). By drawing out your image, you're giving yourself a motivational picture to mentally hold onto to get to the end of your goal:

— CHAPTER ROUND-UP —

☑ Splice your goal down into weekly **goal steps**.

☑ Find consistent **accountability** for completing goals.

☑ Track your daily **goal progress** in your **Goal Tracker**.

☑ Emotionally connect with each **goal marker**.

☑ Practice the feelings you want to feel.

CHAPTER 5

When You Want to Feel Calm and Confident...

* The Decision Tracker
* The Word Selector
* The Frustration Surfboard

* The Calm Center
* The Good Stuff Journal

THE DECISION TRACKER

Decision fatigue is a type of mental exhaustion that can happen when you have to make too many small choices all in a row. When decision fatigue gets cranked up a notch from anxiety and stress, it can turn into **decision paralysis,** which feels like you're "frozen" between choices. And instead of moving forward, you just drive yourself around and around in an anxiety loop.

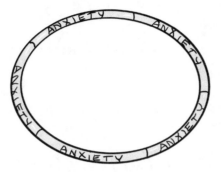

A decision paralysis loop sounds something like this: *Should I go this way or that way? I want to go this way, but the other way is better. Maybe I should just go this way. Or maybe that way is better... Or maybe it isn't better... Maybe I should go the other way...(repeat four times)...*

Sometimes, the seemingly small everyday decision we have to make is not necessarily a serious one, but we still find ourselves completely unable to make up our minds in this frustrating state.

Have you ever gone out to eat with someone and watched as they couldn't choose what to order because they were stuck in a decision loop between two menu items (as the waiter watched in anguish)? Have you ever waited for hours for someone to pick an outfit to wear because they couldn't seem to settle on one (even after they'd emptied out their closet a few dozen times)? Chances are, you've not only witnessed loops like these, you've also probably been stuck in a few yourself.

Usually, what's getting us stuck here is a thought like: "I am not going to make the perfect decision, and it's going to be a disaster!"

This goes back to **all or nothing** thinking, which can frequently trip us up: We put too much pressure on ourselves to be "perfect" at decision-making, which tanks our **decision-making confidence** altogether, causing us to not make any decisions at all.

Change Your Decision Self-Talk

To strengthen this decision-making confidence, start by practicing positive **micro-thoughts** each time you make a small decision:

"I am making a good enough decision based on the information I have in front of me."

"If this doesn't work out, I will be able to figure out what the next step will be."

"If I make a decision and I don't like it, I can always make future decisions to change things."

Having decision-making confidence means that if the option you chose doesn't work out, you believe in your own ability to adjust things later.
      You can remember it like this:

In order to build up your decision-making confidence,

practice believing in your own ability

to fix things in the future.

In other words, you have the ability to solve problems if they happen to occur. You just might not fully *believe* this about yourself just yet.
      It can be helpful to remember:

Anxiety often convinces us that we can't figure things out.

But we are figuring things out. Every single day!

Using The Decision Tracker

I came up with **The Decision Tracker** to help boost people's decision-making confidence by getting them to realize that they're actually making small decisions every day that are working out already. To use this tool, as you go throughout your day, start to notice the small decisions you're making as you make them, and keep track of them in a notebook.

Notice the Small Things

Let's say you just picked a nice breakfast to eat. Mentally take note that you just made a good small decision. You found a new car mechanic to take your car to for an oil change—notice how you made that decision and that it worked out okay. You found a new route home that saved you time. Mentally note that decision after you make it.

Then, write down on a list all the decisions you're making that have worked out well for you. Update it each week as you make more decisions, and actively read your list every time you start to feel that uncomfortable **decision paralysis** kick in.

Using your **Decision Tracker**, you would write something like this out:

Good decisions I have made:

* I chose a nice meal.
* I found a great car mechanic.
* I discovered a new route home that saves time.

By actively observing that you're making small decisions every day, you will ramp up your decision-making confidence to make even bigger decisions later on.

As your **decision-tracking list** really starts to grow in length, you will be proving to your own brain that you *are* making decisions all the time, that these decisions *often* work out for you, and that you *will continue* to make good decisions in the future.

Worksheet: Write it out!

In order to boost our decision-making confidence, let's start by keeping track of small everyday decisions we make that work out well for us (for example: You chose a nice restaurant that ended up being delicious; you found a good mechanic; you found a new place to visit that was fun).

Every week, try to add a few more daily decisions to this list. See if you can get to 10!

1. . . . .

2. . . . .

3. . . . .

4. . . . .

5. . . . .

6. . . . .

7. . . . .

8. . . . .

9. . . . .

10. . . . .

THE WORD SELECTOR

When we have a task to do, our own words can sometimes get in our way, blocking our path. As you learned from **The Wall Crusher**, the words you choose to say to yourself are important, because we can easily trigger our own wall of mental resistance with what we say.

And yet, every day, we say negative phrases to ourselves about tasks we have to do, without ever thinking how these words are emotionally affecting us and how they are affecting our ability to do the tasks we're talking about.

Have you ever waited in a long line somewhere and thought something like, "This line is killing me!" or "I hate this line! It's the worst ever!" Or perhaps you hated doing an assignment and you thought, "I am sick and tired of doing this!" or "This is my worst nightmare!"

Most likely, the line isn't "killing" you, it's probably not making you "sick," and chances are, you don't even really "hate" it. These are just strong hyperboles we learn to throw around as a pattern of speech.

When we're feeling frustrated, stressed, or burnt-out, there is a tendency to negatively exaggerate things we just don't feel like doing. We hear these types of harsh exaggerated phrases uttered all the time by other people during everyday situations, but how are these phrases actually affecting our brains when we say them to ourselves?

It's helpful to remember:

Your brain is always listening to the words you tell it.

Your brain doesn't necessarily hear the sarcasm, intended humor, or even the theatrical effect of the exaggeration. Your brain hears stressful words like "nightmare," and "the worst ever," and then it responds accordingly… with stress.

> **Neuroscience nugget:** In a recent study, participants were asked to exaggerate their reactions while watching a video that was designed to elicit emotional responses. The participants who were asked to exaggerate their negative reactions to the video experienced higher heart rates and cardiovascular stress compared to the group that watched the video in a normal "watching" state (Demaree *et al.*, 2004).

In other words, saying stressful phrases to yourself just might be triggering a stress response in your body, which then makes your brain feel like doing the task even less. So, if we want to actually improve our ability to complete a task or goal, it can be helpful to start changing how we are speaking about the task or goal in front of us.

Speak Like You're Listening

* Watch your words as you say them. You don't have to change them right away; just pause, and let the words sit for a second after they come out of your mouth. Let them hang in the air above your head like a cartoon speech bubble.
* Label the words. When you hear what you've just said, add a label

to them. For instance, if you catch yourself saying, "This task is killing me!" pause, and then add: "Wow, that was a really **harsh** thing to say."

* Use **The Word Selector** to pick a new phrase.

Just the Facts

One way to think about how to re-word your self-talk is to **just state the facts**. On the classic TV show *Dragnet*, Sgt. Joe Friday would often interrupt a chatty witness by bluntly stating: "All we want are the facts, ma'am!" which later got misquoted into the memorable catchphrase "Just the facts, ma'am" (Webb, 1951).

Just like Sgt. Joe Friday, state "just the facts" to yourself when you catch yourself exaggerating in a negative way.

Example: "I'm so sick and tired of this work review!"

Pause. Delete. Just the facts.

Word editor: "Finishing this review is a somewhat difficult task I am doing at the moment."

While we haven't replaced it with a new positive statement yet, at least we're just stating the feeling without the unnecessary negative exaggeration.

Example: "If I have to wait in this long line another minute, I will die."

Pause. Delete. Just the facts.

Word editor: "This is a very long line and I'm feeling a little restless."

Acknowledging what you're feeling is perfectly okay to do. When we fully acknowledge and accept where we're at emotionally, we can then begin to shift what we're feeling to a calmer place.

To remember this, try this equation:

$$\text{Stating the facts} = \text{Reduces resistance and anxiety}$$

The Advanced Word Selector

Now, let's try **The Advanced Word Selector** by adding a new and improved phrase to our self-talk:

Example: "I am sick to death of this project!"

Word Selector: "This is a new project and it's taking me a little time to figure it all out."

Advanced Word Selector: "But even so, I will probably be able to finish it by tomorrow, and then I can feel good that I've completed it."

Example: "I hate doing the dishes! It's the absolute worst!"

Word Selector: "I am not enjoying this cleaning task right now. However, it will be much nicer to look at the kitchen once the dishes are done."

Advanced Word Selector: "Having the dishes put away will allow me to relax and enjoy the rest of the evening. I wonder what I will do next that will be more fun?"

So, the next time you're scrubbing the sink while grumbling to yourself… Pause. Listen. Hear what you are saying. And then, scrub away at the words that make you feel bad…until they make you feel better.

Worksheet: Write it out!

Throughout the week, try to catch yourself when you say something that's a negative exaggeration (e.g., "This is a nightmare!"). Then, edit the phrase down to **just the facts** (e.g., "This assignment is taking me longer than usual") and add a more positive phrase that might help you complete it (e.g., "I'm going to feel so relieved when it's done").

A common negative phrase I hear myself say:

. . . .

. . . .

. . . .

. . . .

Rewrite the phrase, stating "just the facts":

. . . .

. . . .

. . . .

. . . .

Now, rewrite the phrase into a more positive helpful statement:

. . . .

. . . .

. . . .

. . . .

☆

THE FRUSTRATION SURFBOARD

What happens when we're stuck doing a task that's become so *frustrating* that we can't remember how to pick better words using **The Word Selector**? Maybe you've gone into **hyperfocus** mode for too long because you haven't taken any **Time Buffer breaks,** or maybe you've jumped too far ahead with a goal and overwhelmed yourself too fast. Now, frustration is on the rise, and it feels like you've "jammed" your mental gears, grinding any motion to a screeching halt!

Since frustration can feel like a mix of two intense emotions—anger and overwhelm—it can sometimes be a tricky feeling to navigate your way out of.

Neuroscience nugget: Researchers at the University of Washington recently discovered how nociception neurons, which are sometimes referred to as "frustration neurons," can affect dopamine in our brains. These "frustration neurons" get activated when we're frustrated, and they release nociception, a molecule that suppresses dopamine. Dopamine makes us feel pleasure, motivation, and rewards (Micu, 2019).

In other words, to our brains, feeling *frustrated* is the opposite of feeling *motivated*. When we feel frustrated, we can't also feel motivated. That's why it's a good idea when you're frustrated to find ways to reset yourself and bring the stress down, so that you can find your motivation again.

Ride the Frustration Out

Frustration is an uncomfortable and intense feeling that often triggers an internal tirade from our inner critic. Often when people get frustrated, their inner critic starts chiming in: "Why can't I figure this out? What's wrong with me? What's my problem anyway?!"

And clearly, this negative self-talk only makes us feel much worse about the situation and ourselves. So, how can we stop this negative cycle at the onset? You can start by using **The Frustration Surfboard** to carry you to calmer shores.

As with most intense feelings, frustration is a like a wave. At the wave's crest, the frustration feels the most intense and unbearable. However, by simply breathing into your frustration, one deep breath at a time, and taking a few quick mental steps to soothe yourself to a calmer place, the crest will start to fall, and you can start to feel relief faster.

Here's how to use **The Frustration Surfboard** the next time you feel those mental gears "jamming up":

* Take a deep breath, and breathe...into...the...frustration, one long breath at a time. Go into the feeling with each deliberate deep breath.
* As you're taking long deep breaths, say to yourself mentally: "Breathing in the calm... Breathing out the frustration." Try doing this for a few minutes.
* Mindfully observe how the frustration starts to subside with each breath until. Feel it leave you...slowly...with...each...deep...breath.
* As you get to the end of the frustration wave, build in a few soothing **micro-thoughts**:

> *"I'm learning how to breathe into my feelings."*
>
> *"I'm getting good at navigating my way through this emotion."*
>
> *"I'm practicing new ways of getting through this feeling."*
>
> *"All feelings are temporary. This one will end soon."*
>
> *"I'm riding this feeling out one breath at a time."*

Ride out the frustration wave—by taking long deep breaths and telling yourself soothing, gentle phrases that calm you down. Chances are, the frustration will only last a few (intense) minutes this way. After that, you can decide to let the feeling go. Watch it as it passes. Notice how you can simply let it subside by breathing the feeling out one deep breath at a time.

Then, you can make the clear decision not to get back on the surfboard and ride the same wave of frustration all over again. Free up your headspace for more enjoyable feelings ahead.

Worksheet: Color it out!

Use your creativity to color **The Frustration Surfboard** below, and write out a few soothing **micro-thoughts** you can tell yourself the next time you feel frustrated:

. . . .

. . . .

THE CALM CENTER

After the frustration wave passes, it's helpful to step away from the task you were doing for a while to calm down and ground yourself before proceeding. Stepping away from a frustrating problem for a moment often provides the clarity you were seeking to solve it. Sometimes, changing locations, putting away your phone for a short time, or even stepping outside for a few minutes can get you to a clearer mental perspective much faster.

It can be helpful to remember:

After you calm down a little,
you will be able to finish the task ahead
in a clearer and easier way.

Imagine a **large ocean rock** that waves pass over constantly. The ocean rock is your **Calm Center**. Let the waves of emotion come and go, washing over you. Like a rock, you are grounded in your own inner strength and calmness. When you connect with your **Calm Center**, it's much easier to get things done.

You can think of it like this:

*When you find your Calm Center,
time becomes your friend, not your enemy.*

Feeling calm is what stretches our perception of time. Feeling frustrated and stressed-out is what shrinks our perception of time. And our perception of time changes constantly depending on our emotional states. That's why it's beneficial to practice finding your calm so that you can create more time for yourself to enjoy.

During a time when you are not feeling frustrated, practice connecting with your **Calm Center**. Sit somewhere, breathe into it, feel what calm actually feels like for a few minutes. What does calm actually feel like in your body and brain? How long can you stay there before it gets uncomfortable? Stretch the feeling out a little bit at a time. Every time you practice, you will be able to stay there a little longer.

Grounding Techniques

Using **mindfulness, grounding techniques** are quick ways to "ground" yourself in the **present moment,** which helps you find your **Calm Center** faster. Here are a few grounding techniques to choose from. Try to find one that works for your particular brain:

* Imagine a large ocean rock. Picture yourself as this ocean rock. The waves crash into it and pass over it, but it remains steady, strong and unchanging. Breathe into this visualization for as long as you can sustain it. Imagine your breaths to be like the waves passing over the rock. Stay with this visualization for a few minutes if you can.
* Hold a small object in your hands and feel how it feels to hold: Is it cold, is it warm, is it round, or smooth? List five adjectives that describe

the object in your hands as you take a few deep breaths. Focusing our senses on a small object can help anchor us in the present moment more. When we're anchored in the present moment, our stress and anxiety levels will naturally start to come down.

* For a few minutes, focus on feeling the energy in the tips of your fingers on one hand. Can you feel little points of energy in your fingertips? How long can you focus your attention there? How warm and tingly can you make them feel? Make the warm tingly feeling grow in intensity. Try to move that energy from one hand to another, and then once both hands are tingling, move the energy all the way down to your feet. Try to stay with this feeling until it naturally fades away.

* Breathe in and tense up your shoulders, your fists, and your muscles on purpose for four seconds. Hold for four seconds. Then, let exhale the breath out for six seconds and let everything relax all at once. Do this a few times in a row, each time letting go of even more tension with each exhale.

* Lie on the floor. Place your hands on your stomach and make your hands rise and fall with each breath you take. Imagine underneath your hands is a bright white circle of energy, and every time you breathe, it expands out to become an even bigger and brighter circle. How big can you make that bright white circle in your imagination with your breathing? Take a few seconds at the end of this visualization, to picture the bright white circle growing so big that it encompasses your entire body, filling you with a sense of calm and peace.

Pick a few different ways to practice finding your **Calm Center** a little each day. Get to know what it feels like there more of the time. The more you get to know what it feels like, the easier it will be to access it when you need to visit it again. Practice finding your Calm Center during non-stressful times and you'll be able to find it faster during the stressful times. Practice feeling calm, and the calm feeling will only grow as a result. After a while, you will no longer have to remember to find your **Calm Center**; it will start finding you.

THE GOOD STUFF JOURNAL

To close out this book of tools, I want to leave you with a powerful exercise to fully appreciate all of the good stuff you're doing to move yourself in a positive direction.

Once you've formed some new habits to set goals, stay focused, and feel more motivated, you will now have one place to write down everything you've been doing that's been working out for you.

The **Good Stuff Journal** is a way to get our brains to notice all the good stuff that happens each day. It's also a way to fuse all the knowledge you've gained from this book into one place that you can enjoy reading and reviewing on a regular basis.

Write the Good Stuff Down

Pick out a small journal that feels good to you to write in. Make sure it is a separate one if you are using journals for other things. Using **The Color Coder,** pick a color that makes you feel happy. Pick a pen that feels nice to write with, too. Make it feel like a very special and fun experience to use this particular journal.

As a nightly ritual, write down 3–10 things in your **Good Stuff Journal** that made you feel good. That's all you have to do! Super easy!

Whether it's stuff you're proud of, **Time Buffers** you remembered to take, **high-intensity tasks** you completed, **goal markers** you've reached, **walls of resistance** you crushed, **Stuff Stations** you created, decisions from your **Decision Tracker, calm moments** you connected with, or **motivational**

micro-thoughts you told yourself, put all of it in your **Good Stuff Journal**… every single day.

The secret of this tool is that you have to use it daily in order to feel the full positive effects. When you're writing things down, just stick with the good stuff. It's called the **Good Stuff Journal** for a reason! Save the other types of stuff for other types of journals, ones where you are processing other emotions and free-writing. For this particular tool, we're fully focusing on things that are working out for you right here, right now.

There are truly are lots of things working out for you right now. It's just a matter of taking a few minutes to pause, look around, and fully see them.

In other words:

Become a witness to your own good things.

Remember the Good Stuff

Once a week, read through your **Good Stuff Journal**. Start at the beginning and flip through it and let yourself fully enjoy everything you've written down.

Let your brain fully take in how many good things there are on the pages before you. Reading your pages will make you realize that you're actually making progress.

You'll observe where you started at the beginning of your journal and you'll see how far you've travelled.

In fact, you'll become your own **goal sponsor**. And then, you'll just want to keep on going!

You'll realize that you really are getting to where you want to go, one small step at a time.

— CHAPTER ROUND-UP —

☑ Keep track of the **good decisions** you have made.

☑ Your brain is always listening to the words you use.

☑ Ride out frustration one deep breath at a time.

☑ Practice connecting to your **Calm Center** each day.

☑ Become a witness to your own **good things**.

Mental Health Resources

ADHD Resources

ADDitude Magazine: www.additudemag.com/category/adhd-add

CHADD (Children and Adults with Attention-Deficit/ Hyperactivity Disorder): https://chadd.org

ADHD Self-Test: https://add.org/adhd-test

Dr. Hallowell, ADHD podcast and videos: https://drhallowell.com

Psychotherapist Directories in the USA

Psychology Today: http://psychologytoday.com

Therapy Den: http://therapyden.com

Psychotherapist Directories in the UK

NHS: www.nhs.uk/service-search/find-a-psychological-therapies-service

Counselling Directory: www.counselling-directory.org.uk

Anxiety and Mental Health Resources

ADAA (Anxiety & Depression Association of America): https://adaa.org

American mental health hotlines/NAMI (National Alliance on Mental Illness): www.nami.org/Support-Education/NAMI-HelpLine/Top-HelpLine-Resources

Anxiety UK: www.anxietyuk.org.uk

Mind helpline: www.mind.org.uk/information-support/helplines

Mental Health Charities

Attention Deficit Disorder Organization: https://add.org

Brain & Behavior Research Foundation: www.bbrfoundation.org

References

Altgassen, M., Scheres, A., and Edel, M. A. (2019) "Prospective memory (partially) mediates the link between ADHD symptoms and procrastination." *ADHD: Attention Deficit and Hyperactivity Disorders 11*, 59–71, doi:1007/s12402-018-0273-x

Arnsten, A. F. (2009) "The emerging neurobiology of attention deficit hyperactivity disorder: The key role of the prefrontal association cortex." *The Journal of Pediatrics 154*(5), I–S43. https://doi.org/10.1016/j.jpeds.2009.01.018

Bangma, D. F., Tucha, L., Fuermaier, A. B. M., Tucha, O., and Koerts, J. (2020) "Financial decision-making in a community sample of adults with and without current symptoms of ADHD." *PLOS ONE 15*(10), e0239343. https://doi.org/10.1371/journal. pone.0239343

Bess, G. and Briggins, J. (2016) "Here's what Olympic athletes listen to before they compete for the Gold." *Vice*, August 3. www.vice.com/en/article/wnyzjx/ rio-olympics-athlete-warm-up-playlist-canada

Brice, R. (2019) "A User's Guide: I have ADHD, So Why Am I So Exhausted?" *Healthline*, August 1. www.healthline.com/health/ADHD/adhd-fatigue

Cherry, K. (2019) "How listening to music can have psychological benefits." *Very Well Mind*, December 10. www.verywellmind.com/surprising-psychological-benefits-of-music-4126866

Cole, S., Balcetis, E., and Zhang, S. (2013) "Visual perception and regulatory conflict: Motivation and physiology influence distance perception." *Journal of Experimental Psychology 142*(1), 18–22. https://pubmed.ncbi.nlm.nih.gov/22449101

Contreras, C. M. and Gutiérrez-Garcia, A. G. (2018) "Cortisol awakening response: An ancient adaptive feature." *Journal of Psychiatry and Psychiatric Disorders 2*, 29–40. https://www.fortunejournals.com/articles/cortisol-awakening-response-an-ancient-adaptive-feature.html

Creswell, J. D., Dutcher, J. M., Klein, W. M., Harris, P. R., and Levine, J. M. (2013) "Self-affirmation improves problem-solving under stress." *PLOS ONE 8*(5), e62593. https://doi.org/10.1371/journal.pone.0062593

Dawson, J. and Sleek, S. (2018) "The fluidity of time: Scientists uncover how emotions alter time perception." *Psychological Science*, September 28. www.psychologicalscience.org/observer/the-fluidity-of-time

Demaree, H. A., Schmeichel, B. J., and Robinson, J. L. (2004) "Behavioral, affective and physiological effects of negative and positive emotional exaggeration." *Cognition and Emotion 18*(8), 1079–1097. http://gruberpeplab.com/teaching/psych231_fall2013/documents/231_Demaree2004.pdf

Dodson, W. (2021) "The secrets of the ADHD Brain." *ADDitude Magazine*, July 27. www.additudemag.com/secrets-of-the-adhd-brain

Habermeyer, S. (2021) "Music that focuses the brain." *ADDitude Magazine*, May 5. www.additudemag.com/study-music-to-focus-the-adhd-brain

Hallowell, E. (2005) "Overloaded circuits: Why smart people underperform." *Harvard Business Review*, January. https://hbr.org/2005/01/overloaded-circuits-why-smart-people-underperform

Hannibal, K. E. and Bishop, M. D. (2014) "Chronic stress, cortisol dysfunction and pain: A psychoneuroendocrine rationale for stress management in pain rehabilitation." *Journal of the American Physical Therapy Association*, July 17.

Heid, M. (2015) "You asked: Are my devices messing with my brain?" *Time Magazine*, May 13. https://time.com/3855911/phone-addiction-digital-distraction

Jabr, F. (2013) "Why your brain needs more downtime." *Scientific American*, October 15. www.scientificamerican.com/article/mental-downtime

Katzir, M., Emanuel, A., and Liberman, N. (2020) "Cognitive performance is enhanced if one knows when the task will end." *Cognition 197*, April, 104189. doi:10.1016/j.cognition.2020.104189

Klein, L. (2014) "All you need is love, gratitude and oxytocin." *Greater Good Magazine*, February 11. https://greatergood.berkeley.edu/article/item/love_gratitude_oxytocin

Lackschewitz, H., Hüther, G., and Kröner-Herwig, B. (2008) "Physiological and psychological stress responses in adults with attention-deficit/hyperactivity disorder (ADHD)." *Psychoneuroendocrinology 33*(5), 612–624. https://doi.org/10.1016/j.psyneuen.2008.01.016

Levine, H. (2020) "Meditation and yoga for ADHD." WebMD, January 17. www.webmd.com/add-adhd/adhd-mindfulness-meditation-yoga

McGonigal, K. (2020) "Five surprising ways exercise changes your brain." *Greater Good Magazine*, January 6. https://greatergood.berkeley.edu/article/item/five_surprising_ways_exercise_changes_your_brain

Micu, A. (2019) "Researchers identify neurons that shut down rewards and motivation in the brain of mice." *ZME Science*, July 26. www.zmescience.com/science/nociceptin-neuron-dopamine-155028

Milbrand, L. (2021) "What happens to your brain when you do a puzzle." *Reader's Digest*, September 29. www.rd.com/article/what-happens-to-your-brain-when-do-a-puzzle

Murdock, J. (2020) "Humans have more than 6,000 thoughts per day, psychologists discover." *Newsweek*, July 15. www.newsweek.com/humans-6000-thoughts-every-day-1517963

Murphy, M. (2018) "Neuroscience explains why you need to write down your goals if you actually want to achieve them." Forbes.com, April 15. https://www.forbes.com/sites/markmurphy/2018/04/15/neuroscience-explains-why-you-need-to-write-down-your-goals-if-you-actually-want-to-achieve-them/?sh=6dfe4d379059

Oppong, T. (2017) "Psychological secrets to hack your way to better life habits." *Observer*, March 20. https://observer.com/2017/03/psychological-secrets-hack-better-life-habits-psychology-productivity

Rothbard, N. P. and Wilk, S. L. (2011) "Waking up on the right or wrong side of the bed: Start-of-workday mood, work events, employee affect, and performance." *Academy of Management Journal*, April 4. www.sciencedaily.com/releases/2011/04/110404151353.htm

Shellenbarger, S. (2012) "At work, do headphones really help?" *The Wall Street Journal*, June 7. www.wsj.com/articles/SB10001424052702303395604577432341782110010

Spector, N. (2020) "Doomscrolling is bad for your health. Do this instead." *Today*, August 6. www.today.com/health/how-stop-doomscrolling-its-affect-your-brain-t188725

Thompson, H. (1966) "Quiet murders suit Miss Christie: Visiting writer still prefers to keep crime in family." *The New York Times*, October 27.

Tierney, J. (2011) "Do you suffer from decision fatigue?" *The New York Times Magazine*, August 17. www.nytimes.com/2011/08/21/magazine/do-you-suffer-from-decision-fatigue.html?_r=2

Tuckman, A. (2021) "Are you time blind? 12 ways to use every hour effectively." *ADDitude Magazine*, February 7. www.additudemag.com/slideshows/stop-wasting-time

Umejima, K., Ibaraki, T., Yamazaki, T., and Sakai, K. L. (2021) "Paper notebooks vs. mobile devices: Brain activation differences during memory retrieval." *Frontiers in Behavioral Neuroscience 15*. doi:10.3389/fnbeh.2021.634158

Webb, J. (1951) *Dragnet*. Mark VII Productions, Universal Studios.

Zaki, J. and Mitchell, J. P. (2011) "Equitable decision making is associated with neural markers of intrinsic value." *Proceedings of the National Academy of Sciences 108*(49), 19761–19766. doi:10.1073/pnas.1112324108, www.pnas.org/content/108/49/19761

About the Author

Risa Williams is a licensed clinical therapist with a practice in Los Angeles, specializing in time management and anxiety reduction techniques. She is the author of the self-help books, *The Ultimate Anxiety Toolkit* and *The Ultimate Self-Esteem Toolkit* (JKP Books). She is also a university professor with a background in film and performing arts, and a magazine writer. Read more of her writing at www.risawilliams.com or www.timemanage menttoolkit.com